PRAISE FOR
Prophetic Breakthrough

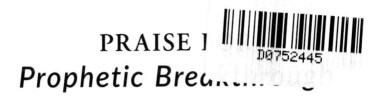

Most believers live without fulfilling their full destiny. Few understand the power of curses and ungodly soul ties. This book, *Prophetic Breakthrough*, will obliterate every demonic hindrance to you walking in your God-given, joyous destiny.

SID ROTH

Host, *It's Supernatural!*

I have personally experienced the dynamic ministry of Hakeem Collins and I can make the following statement with great confidence: what you are about to read is this man's core message. This is what God has entrusted him with in this hour. Hakeem is an emerging prophetic voice who ministers with great passion, fire, and receptivity to the Holy Spirit, and *Prophetic Breakthrough* is the wonderful overflow of his prophetic ministry.

Prophetic Breakthrough is an experience unlike any other. It is a prophetic devotional that positions you to live *daily* on the offense against the powers of darkness. After all, God did not give you His power tools—the Word of God, the Holy Spirit and His gifts, the keys of the Kingdom, etc.—to always be responding and reacting to the devil and his devices. You were made for more, and this devotional gives you the ability to have the winning edge. Hakeem's encouraging, prophetic, empowering entries help put new language to your prayers that will empower you to break every hindrance to fulfilling your potential in God and advance boldly into your destiny.

Hakeem will show you how to walk in this *Prophetic Breakthrough*, yes, but his book does not simply conclude with teaching. Truly, this book is *show and tell*. The devotional element gives you 90 days of powerful prophetic activation, offering revelatory daily encouragements, dynamic declarations, and prayers that will loose God's blessings and cancel the assignments of darkness!

Larry Sparks
Publisher, Destiny Image
Author of *Breakthrough Faith: Living a Life Where Anything Is Possible* and co-author of *The Fire That Never Sleeps*

Dr. Hakeem has done it again! Another explosive book dealing with breakthrough! His revelation on the power of decreeing will totally transform you to break off all soul ties and open the door for divine breakthrough. If you find your mouth cursing your life, this book is for you! Well written and very anointed!

Dr. Jeremy Lopez
CEO of www.identitynetwork.net
Prophetic Resource Website

Dr. Hakeem Collins is a cutting-edge apostolic and prophetic leader who has been given a mandate to prepare the Church for this next wave of spiritual engagement and victory. *Prophetic Breakthrough* is more than a 90-day devotional; it is manual that engages end-time believers as we continue to establish the Kingdom of God and the agenda of the Lamb. This book should be mandatory reading for those who are engaged in training prophets, intercessors, and maturing believers who are ready to live victoriously in Christ. This book will engage your mind and transform your life.

Apostle Damian A. Hinton, Sr.
Apostolic Overseer
The Apostolic Network of International Churches and Ministries

Let me begin by saying that *Prophetic Breakthrough* is not just your ordinary and average book on the prophetic and breakthrough. While there is a genuine hunger rising in the hearts of a generation longing to hear the prophetic heartbeat of the Father, this devotional book is a manual that far exceeds surface prophetic ministry. Written by my dear friend, a powerful apostolic and prophetic voice in the Kingdom, Dr. Hakeem Collins teaches the reader by the Spirit of God to know the power of the prophetic, their decrees, and how it so closely ties into seeing God's plan of breakthrough and delivering power unleashed. Jesus did not leave behind a powerless church but a powerful church who will wield the power and the authority granted to them in the Holy Spirit. Dr. Hakeem beautifully ties in and builds a bridge between the prophetic and how we as the Body of Christ can do just that by speaking, decreeing, and praying God's will from Heaven to earth in our lives. Get ready to not only receive breakthrough but also to be activated into a much deeper level in the prophetic to the glory of God.

Kevin Stevens
Apostolic and Prophetic Revivalist
Greater Glory Ministries
Pastor, Greater Glory Revival Center

Dr. Hakeem Collins' groundbreaking book *Prophetic Breakthrough*, when practically applied daily, will become a master tool in the believer's spiritual toolbox of prayer to break through unbreakable and unhinged situations, circumstances, and resistance. I believe this book will release the necessary supernatural faith needed to those who feel like the paralyzed man in the Bible who couldn't get to Jesus due to the crowd but four men carried him to the rooftop and broke through for the man to get to Jesus for his personal breakthrough.

In Mark 2:4 it says "when they had broken through." They had to break through despite the impossible opposition and create an opening for the paralyzed man to receive his miracle. Dr. Hakeem's book *Prophetic Breakthrough* is a must-read for anyone who may feel spiritually stagnant in their faith or walk with God and desire to operate in and access the power of God. There are prophetic promises that one will have to dig for and others one will have to create through the power of their decrees.

This timely book will become like those four men and will carry and activate the faith of the reader daily to break the limitations that have kept them bound, stuck, and spiritually complacent. Moreover, this book provides the Holy Spirit antidote with power in breaking and shattering invisible, invincible glass ceilings in one's way and life.

I highly recommend this literary work for anyone who desires to see mountains move, glass ceilings cracked, and illegal curses of the enemy broken by the power of their prophetic decrees, which will unleash divine blessings and open the heavens for the reader to experience total victory, freedom, and breakthroughs daily in Christ.

Dr. Naim Collins
President, Fan the Flames Global Ministries
Naim Collins Ministries
www.naimcollinsministries.com

We are honored to highly endorse Dr. Hakeem Collins' newest book release, *Prophetic Breakthrough*. This book is a must-read for anyone serious about fulfilling their prophetic destiny as manifested in the now.

With poignant insight, Dr. Collins takes us on a journey of not only identifying the causes of curses but of how to wage warfare on those chains that shackle us, thus enabling us to obtain real freedom. *"If the son therefore shall make you free, ye shall be free indeed"* (John 8:36 KJV).

Additionally, Dr. Collins walks us through breaking curses and releasing blessings, as well as activating the reader with a 90-day devotional. Read the book today and be finished once and for all with any hindrances to achieving God's best for you!

It's time to empower your breakthrough when you partner with the Holy Spirit and decree your future with wisdom and insight!

Allen and Francine Fosdick
Founders, People of Prophetic Power Ministries, poppm.org
Up Front in the Prophetic, Radio/TV, upfrontintheprophetic.com

Prophetic Breakthrough by Dr. Hakeem Collins is packaged based on the insight and experiences of the author. You can open your world to deep mysteries that give answers to long-standing issues of your life. Never forget that each encounter with destiny comes on the platform of accessing those whom God has put a word in their mouth for you. This is your moment to seize the reins, decrees, and prophetic declarations that take your breakthrough to a place of fulfillment.

RENE PICOTA

Lead Pastor, Streams of Life Church

www.streamsoflifechurch.tv

When Jesus died for our sins, He also broke every sin-ignited curse in our life! Right? Still, we often can't seem to break free from the sins of our past or even the sins of our forefathers. If that's you, don't be discouraged! There is an answer for you in this book. Dr. Hakeem Collins' *Prophetic Breakthrough* is a thorough teaching, a process, and a daily prophetic prayer that addresses these kinds of struggles. It incorporates strategic decrees to break every curse still at large in your life and then activates every blessing that Jesus paid the price for you to have. It incorporates sound teaching, is biblically based, and is undeniably powerful from the first decreeing prayer to the last. This book spoke life to me, and it will do the same for you! You'll definitely revisit its pages again and again.

JENNIFER EIVAZ

Executive pastor, Harvest Christian Center

Turlock, California

Author of *The Intercessor's Handbook*

Most people agree that they need a breakthrough but few know how to receive it! Hakeem Collins provides the promise and power of God's Word and voice to experience the breakthrough you have been waiting for. This book is personal, powerful, and practical. All you need is a key to open your door of breakthrough, and *Prophetic Breakthrough* is full of keys!

DR. LEIF HETLAND

President, Global Mission Awareness

Author of *Giant Slayers, Seeing Through Heaven's*

Eyes and *Healing the Orphan Spirit*

I am a firm believer in saying decrees out loud. I first began Decreeing scriptures out loud as I would walk around the park each day during a challenging time in my life. Some days I would wonder if it was making any impact. Looking back, I can tell you with full confidence it has! Equip yourself with the revelation and rich substance this book has to offer you during this time of your life. God has messengers that release certain books during certain seasons for a reason. Now is your season! Don't go through your next season of your life without this book *Prophetic Breakthrough*.

JOEL YOUNT
Co-founder of Spirit Fuel
www.spiritfuel.me

PROPHETIC BREAK THROUGH

PROPHETIC
BREAK
THROUGH

— DECREES THAT —
BREAK CURSES & RELEASE BLESSINGS

HAKEEM COLLINS

DESTINY IMAGE® PUBLISHERS, INC.

P.O. Box 310, Shippensburg, PA 17257-0310

"Promoting Inspired Lives."

This book and all other Destiny Image and Destiny Image Fiction books are available at Christian bookstores and distributors worldwide.

Cover design by Eileen Rockwell

Interior design by Terry Clifton

For more information on foreign distributors, call 717-532-3040.

Reach us on the Internet: www.destinyimage.com.

ISBN 13 TP: 978-0-7684-1480-6

ISBN 13 eBook: 978-0-7684-1481-3

ISBN 13 HC: 978-0-7684-1642-8

ISBN 13 LP: 978-0-7684-1643-5

For Worldwide Distribution, Printed in the U.S.A.

1 2 3 4 5 6 7 8 / 21 20 19 18 17

DEDICATION

Render therefore to all their dues: tribute to whom tribute is due; custom to whom custom; fear to whom fear; honor to whom honor.

—Romans 13:7 AKJV

With a heart to give honor to who honor is due. I dedicate this book to the King of Glory, Jesus Christ, and the Father who has graced me with a gifted penmanship and the scribe's anointing to communicate, articulate, and prophetically share my heart's message to the world. This book is also dedicated to present and future generations of *prophetic harbingers* that are on the frontlines breaking through to bring about radical change. Finally, I dedicate this book to *you* the reader who has invested your time and resources in this book project and it is my sincere heart's desire and prayer that you are empowered, equipped, and inspired by what you read. I prophesy that this literary work will become the launching pad to perpetual breakthroughs and total victory in Christ Jesus in your life.

ACKNOWLEDGMENTS

Mom—My Queen Paula L. Collins—Thank you for always reminding me of my potential and following up on me, to see that I become all that God has destined me to be. Love you!

Grandmothers—Ruth Collins and Mary Guy—Thank you both for being a continual support and giving me endless wisdom, love, and reassurance that I will be successful if I put my mind to it. I love you guys immensely!

My Twin Brother—Dr. Naim Collins—Thank you for being who you are in my life, a big brother, best friend, confidant, personal prophet, and my James (Son of thunder). You always have my back no matter what and there when I call on you. I am forever grateful that God has chosen you. Love you!

Team of HCM—Prophetess Darlene Tilley (Director of Operations), Elder/Prophetess Sherria Gross (Executive Administrator)—what can I say? Speechless, you guys have been sent by the Father to hold my arms up and keep me accountable. Thanks for putting up with me lol!

Family and friends—Thank you all for your prayers, personal prophecies, love, encouragement, correction, and unwavering support that have catapulted me. I love all of my brothers, sisters, nieces, nephews, uncles, aunts, cousins, god daughter, and HCM ministry covenant partners. Shout out to one of my covenant friend in ministry **Pastor Kevin Stevens,** love you man and thanks for believing in my dream and being one of my greatest supporters.

Spiritual Sons and Daughters—I love each one of you dearly and you are the seal of my apostleship! All of you have a special place in my heart. I am honored and humbled to serve you. Thanks for entrusting me with your lives!

Acquisition Agent of Destiny Image—Sierra White—special love, appreciation and honor goes to you for seeing a diamond in the rough and finding a needle in a haystack. You have been God sent to thrust me as an established author. Thanks for your dear friendship and advocating voice for me to fulfill my authorship dream. I am grateful that it was the timing of the Lord we connected. Love you and thanks again for the opportunity!

Publisher of Destiny Image—Larry Sparks—I want to thank you for seeing the prophetic cry in my heart for this generation and giving me a prophetic voice and platform to deliver my message to the world. You have stretched me in so many ways and your leadership is captivating. Thanks my friend for the push and keeping me relevant to Don Nori Sr's vision for Destiny Image.

Destiny Image Publishers Family—Brad Herman, John Martin, Eileen Rockwell, Christian Rafetto, Meelika Marzzarella, Kyle Loffelmacher, and the entire DI team—Thank you all for being the greatest team on this side of heaven and working diligently to make dreams happen!

CONTENTS

Part One

PROPHETIC BREAKTHROUGH

Chapter One

PROPHETIC VISION FOR BREAKTHROUGH

"Where there is no prophetic vision the people cast off restraint, but blessed is he who keeps the law."

—PROVERB 29:18 ESV

Prophetic Breakthrough is a practical biblical teaching and 90-day devotional book that is aimed to teach you how to recognize seasons of breakthrough and how to obtain breakthrough through obedience to God's Word and voice while breaking curses and illegal soul ties that hinder divine blessings. In addition, its my desire to teach you how to use your spiritual authority to get results and the power of decrees that will move spiritual mountains to fulfill one's God-given calling daily. Many may have heard of the terms *prophetic preaching, prophetic teaching, prophetic evangelism, prophetic worship,* and even *prophetic intercession.* But have we heard of the term *prophetic breakthrough?*

What does that term mean? Before we can answer that question, we must first explore the word *prophecy* and how the prophetic works. *Prophecy* is defined as the function or faculty of prophesying or declaring predictive future events. In simple terms, prophecy is the foretelling or forth-telling of a divinely inspired message by a prophet conveying and articulating through plain communication the heart, mind, and counsel of God to His people.

There is a plethora of great written literature on the topic of prophets, prophecy, and the prophetic ministry or spiritual gifts—much more that is embraced and accepted today than several decades ago. However, even with much revelation and teaching on the prophetic there still exists misunderstanding of its nature, function, and overall biblical purpose. The premise of this book is not to convolute your understanding or knowledge on the prophetic *per se* but to draw a mutual relationship that the prophetic has with breakthrough. Moreover, to explain the importance of prophecy and that it serves as a prophetic advantage to spiritual breakthroughs in every area of a person's life.

If I told you that the ingredient to prophetic breakthrough is in your mouth by prophesying the change you want to see, would you use it? If I told you that the ingredient for you walking into the promises, blessings, favor, and joy of the Lord is *one* word away, would you apply it? If you answered yes, than you are the candidate to see the prophetic words, dreams, and vision of God for your life come to pass. For instance, if you were pulled into a meeting and briefed by a CIA, FBI, or official special armed forces agent and given specific tactics, tools, and intelligence to defeat your enemy, would you comply? I think the answer would be emphatically a yes! God is releasing prophetic decrees over your life, and you can prophesy over your day as well to see the breakthrough you have been believing God to do for you.

As a prophetic leader in the Body of Christ, I have witnessed tremendous breakthroughs, creative miracles, healings, and deliverances through the prophetic word of God. One word from God can and will change everything! I will go further to say that *one prophecy from God not only changes everything but everything about you.* Prophetic ministry is a vital gift today because God has not stopped speaking. As long as there are demons, debt, poverty, sickness, disease, and spiritual strongholds in the lives of believers today, God will always use the prophetic and supernatural as a vehicle to bring divine breakthrough.

God's Promise over You Will Not Be Recalled

Most Christian believers can fall victim to living beneath their full potential in God if they are not aware of their spiritual authority. Consequently, due to ignorance we oftentimes live life in vain, aimless and purposeless. Living amiss and clueless is like rowing a boat without a paddle, which is ineffective; living worthless is a waste of time. God desires for us to live out our Christian walk with an aim and not aimless, with a clue and not clueless. We have to war over our personal prophecies, which are declared from the throne of God. The enemy is waging war over your fulfillment. God's Word circles the universe to find a yielded vessel prepared to be used in the right divine season. It is important to Him that you are ready to receive your dream and prophecy and walk in the fulfillment of it.

Remember, God's Word will not return to Him unfulfilled (see Psalm 55:11). God has a proven track record of accomplishing His Word. The devil wants to see you fall short of your destiny. Your breakthrough in life hangs in the balance between heaven and earth. I am reminded of the prophet Daniel who prayed for a revelation and his prayers to be answered but it was met with resistance in the heavenly places from the princes of Persia.

> He said to me, "O Daniel, man of high esteem, understand the words that I am about to tell you and stand upright, for I have now been sent to you." And when he had spoken this word to me, I stood up trembling. Then he said to me, "Do not be afraid, Daniel, for from the first day that you set your heart on understanding this and on humbling yourself before your God, your words were heard, and I have come in response to your words. But the prince of the kingdom of Persia was withstanding

me for twenty-one days; then behold, Michael, one of the chief princes, came to help me, for I had been left there with the kings of Persia" (Daniel 10:11-13 NASB).

God sent Archangel Michael to assist Gabriel, who was met with much resistance by the princes of Persia, to war on behalf of Daniel's prayer petitions. We must understand that the first time Daniel prayed, God answered him and sent it express mail through Gabriel to deliver it. God summoned Daniel's answer to him, but it was hindered between heaven and earth. In other words, the answers to his prayers were stuck between the first heaven and third heaven.

We can see how important words are to God but also to the kingdom of darkness. Did you know that the greatness of your prophecy could be held up by demonic principalities, opposing forces, and powers in the heavenly realm? God gave Daniel a strategy to release his declared prophecy and answer—Daniel had to live a lifestyle committed to God, prayer, consecration, fasting, and only eating what was ordained of God. What Daniel prayed for and asked of the Lord was restricted and prohibited for three weeks. Daniel's breakthrough was hindered for 21 days.

Days to Breakthrough

Can you imagine how many prayers, blessings, miracles, healings, and prophecies that you have requested from the Lord may be stopped, restricted, hindered, and halted by invisible enemies? Depending on the assignment and prophetic word declared over you, the enemy will do everything in his limited power to keep that word from ever coming into your life. I often say *that the greater the prophecy, the greater the warfare!* I believe that if one's prophecy and declaration from heaven is not initiating warfare of any kind then maybe it is not a true word from the Lord. The number 21 is the number of habit, pattern, revelation, and breakthrough. Gabriel carried Daniel's prayer answer and revelation knowledge, but Archangel

Michael carried the breakthrough power to release it out of the hands of the princes of Persia.

Sometimes your breakthrough and blessing will not just be handed over to you that easily if it is from God. Your breakthrough will always face opposition. The opposition is what God uses to create an opportunity for you. As you read the prophetic daily entries, decrees, declarations, and mediation scriptures—be encouraged that your breakthrough is coming signed, sealed, and stamped with the approval of God. If your breakthrough is meeting resistance, then I suggest that we become like Daniel who matched the resistance with persistence to reach breakthrough. This is what Daniel did in prayer. He was consistent until he got his answer. What are we willing to fight for to see divine breakthrough and change? Daniel fought back by fasting and praying.

Daniel received revelation and his breakthrough in 21 days, and God wants you to receive yours as well. Some prayers may not take that long, but regardless the promises of the Lord are yes and amen. Consider these questions as you read this book. How many personal prophecies that you have received may be held up? Have you ever wondered why your prophecy or dream is taking a long time to be fulfilled? Have you ever wondered why things in your life may not be working out for you as was forecasted? In addition, have you ever considered that things are the way they are because you are the way you are? Have you ever thought why your breakthrough has not come? Moreover, who and what is holding up your divine breakthrough?

I come to encourage you to see in the next 90 days your personal prophecy, dream, and vision beginning to unfold for you. Have you waited on something you were praying for and it never came through? It is not that God does not want you to receive what you have been praying for, but there may be demonic spirits holding up your prayer requests. Keep in mind that what you pray for may not always be in the plan or will of God for your life and destiny. God only moves on His Word and will over your life. However, there are things that the Father feels we are not ready for and will not release until His divine timing. Daniel prayed and God answered him.

When you pray God's will, God will respond. However, the enemy will also respond. God is for you and not against you. There are also many other factors and things that can be holding up your dream, prophetic fulfillment, and breakthrough. Things such as sin, generational curses, deception, unforgiveness, witchcrafts against you, illegal soul ties, false agreements, disobedience, ignorance, and our own rebellious decisions. I have placed in this book prophetic breakthrough decrees and declarations for you to read aloud with authority that will break life curses and release Heaven's answers of breakthrough for you. It is my heart and desire to see *you* walk out the dreams of Heaven and break the nightmares of the past or present. I have written this book with *you* in heart and in mind.

Ignorance: The Enemy of the Believer

Timothy was reassured and reminded by his apostolic father Paul of his prophetic charge and commissioning, his assignment in the apostolic calling. Timothy was commissioned by Paul to war against the enemy with his personal prophecies. His prophetic word becomes a weapon against the enemy. The enemy is after your prophecies, dreams, visions, and burdens from God, so you have to take them and use them as a sword against the enemy. We must have the prophetic advantage over the enemy and use what God has declared to wage a good warfare. Timothy was encouraged to commit to the work that was given to him by his personal prophecy. We must understand that our prophecy, a word from God, will incite warfare from the enemy.

If it is a true word of purpose and destiny from God, the devil will try to stop you. Our prophetic words will serve as a battling axe and ram in the spirit to allow us to withstand resistance, error, and any curses that come because of being obedient to God in our life's charge and calling. There is a saying, "What you do not know will not hurt you." I beg to differ on this because the Bible is clear that God's people are *destroyed for of lack of knowledge"* (Hos. 4:6 NASB). It does not say destroyed by poverty, sickness, disease, demons, or debt but due to lack of knowledge.

Ignorance will always be the opposition of the believer. We defeat the enemy by the Word of God and applying it in our lives. The greatest enemy and weapon against God's people is not sickness, poverty, disease, and demons, but it is this simple word called "ignorance." If the enemy can keep God's people blind and deceived of the truth of God's Word and prophetic promises concerning them than he can allow them to rob themselves from truly being liberated and blessed.

Binding and Loosing Powers

I love what the Bible declares in Matthew 18:17-19:

> *If he refuses to listen to them, tell it to the church; and if he refuses to listen even to the church, let him be to you as a Gentile and a tax collector. Truly I say to you, whatever you bind on earth shall have been bound in heaven; and whatever you loose on earth shall have been loosed in heaven. Again I say to you, that if two of you agree on earth about anything that they may ask, it shall be done for them by My Father who is in heaven* (NASB).

As spirit-filled believers in the New Covenant church, through the Holy Spirit we have been giving binding and loosing privileges. We have been given authority through the Holy Spirit and the Word of God to judge and prohibit unlawful, ungodly activities and permit lawful, godly activities. In other words, we can prohibit demonic activities and unlawful acts and patterns in our lives and permit godly practices and moral and righteous patterns in our lives. We can disallow sin, unrighteousness, curses, demonic influences, etc. and allow blessings, righteous acts, and godly influences.

As we know, the term *binding* and *loosing* was originally a Jewish phrase appearing in the New Testament. Its particular usage, to bind and to loose, simply means to forbid by an indisputable authority and to permit by an indisputable authority. Binding and loosing was adopted by Jesus and was given to His apostles. Later, this binding and loosing was adopted by the New Testament believers in the church. We have kingdom authority in Christ to exercise our spiritual rights. As spirit-filled believers, we have been given power over the works of the enemy(see Luke 10:19).

Moreover, through the Word of God we can prohibit and forbid curses and any ungodliness from entering our lives, while standing on the promises of God. What are we allowing to enter our lives? Why are we not using our spiritual authority to address root issues and things in our lives? We know that *"the blessing of the Lord makes one rich, and He adds no sorrow with it"* (Prov. 10:22 NKJV). It is time to dispel and repel things in our lives that are not in our best interests or in the will of God and release divine favor, blessings, and opportunities.

We must use our authority as believers standing on God's Word, knowing that *"whatever you bind on earth shall have been bound in heaven; and whatever you loose on earth shall have been loosed in heaven"* (Matt. 18:18 NASB). Heaven will back you up when *you* are speaking as the Holy Spirit leads *you*. I want to stir you up to disallow what God disallows and permit what God permits in your life. Heaven has your spiritual dashboard where the Holy Spirit becomes the indicator and compass in your life to steer and drive your dreams forward as you comply with His leading. Release Heaven on earth through the Word of God repealing and replacing hell's agenda with Heaven's agenda and purpose.

Ask for the Rain

Your prophetic breakthrough is held up and God wants to release the rain to break any spiritual drought. Elijah knew how to pray and summon God's provision in a season of spiritual famine. He did not have to work magic or anything of that sort, but through a right covenant with the God of Heaven, who is the Father, the rain showers came to him. Heaven has floodgates and doors that can be unlocked and opened. There are storehouses of blessings, breakthroughs, and miracles that God wants to rain down upon His people. His Word is like rain that releases the floodgates to soak those who are experiencing a spiritual famine or in a desolate place. What summoned the cloud? Prayer summoned his prophetic breakthrough of rain supernaturally. God gave the prophet Elijah a key and principle to unlock the invisible resources into the visible realm.

If a prophet prayed, prophesied, and called for the judgment of God to deliver a famine in the land, then the same prophet was instrumental in releasing the rain as well. Where in your life might you have caused a spiritual famine, lack, or drought to occur? Are there any dry places that you can think of that are keeping you from swimming in the pools of Heaven here on earth? There are many droughts and personal famines in our lives that God wants to end and cause us to embark on a new day and season. The prophet released the rain by asking for it in prayer. Revival and breakthrough come through prayer, fasting, and loyalty to God and His Word. We can ask for the rain from Heaven and God will release it. Elijah saw the answer to his prayer come in a cloud in due season and it was the kairos (opportune season of God) and timing for the drought to end.

After a three-and-half-year famine, Elijah prayed fervently and consistently seven times to see the dew of Heaven come in a cloud that looked like a man's hand releasing the rain. God wants to open the heavens over you to release the rain of blessing in your life, family, ministry, church, business, city, region, and nation. Heaven is pregnant with your breakthrough, and the water valves are about to break and burst forth as you read the devotionals and pray the decrees set forth each day for 90 days. There is an invisible battle going on around you that is contending against your destiny, and we must put on the whole armor of God daily to fight back with the Word of God. I love what Ephesians 6:11-13 says:

> *Put on the full armor of God, so that you will be able to stand firm against the schemes of the devil. For our struggle is not against flesh and blood, but against the rulers, against the powers, against the world forces of this darkness, against the spiritual forces of wickedness in the heavenly places. Therefore, take up the full armor of God, so that you will be able to resist in the evil day, and having done everything, to stand firm* (NASB).

This is a spiritual battle over your breakthrough and not a natural or fleshly one. The Bible declares clearly in Second Corinthians 10:3-5:

> *For though we walk in the flesh, we do not war according to the flesh, for the weapons of our warfare are not of the flesh, but divinely powerful for the destruction of fortresses. We are destroying speculations and every lofty thing raised up against the knowledge of God, and we are taking every thought captive to the obedience of Christ* (NASB).

Daily Benefits of Breakthrough

Let us take a look at the benefits of the spoken Word of the Lord and the power that it possesses. We must understand that God's spoken Word is more powerful than we can ever imagine if we trust and believe by faith that we can speak change and daily walk in total obedience as outlined in God's Word.

God's Word will sharpen you and help to reach breakthrough:

> *For the word of God is living and active and sharper than any two-edged sword, and piercing as far as the division of soul and spirit, of both joints and marrow, and able*

to judge the thoughts and intentions of the heart. And there is no creature hidden from His sight, but all things are open and laid bare to the eyes of Him with whom we have to do (Hebrews 4:12-13 NASB).

God's Word will tear down, destroy, overthrow, build, and plant:

See, today I appoint you over nations and kingdoms to uproot and tear down, to destroy and overthrow, to build and to plant (Jeremiah 1:10 NIV).

God's Word brings revival, reformation, restoration, and revitalization:

"Is not my word like fire," declares the Lord, "and like a hammer that breaks a rock in pieces?" (Jeremiah 23:29 NIV)

God's Word coupled with fasting will break curses and loose bands:

Is it a fast like this which I choose, a day for a man to humble himself? Is it for bowing one's head like a reed and for spreading out sackcloth and ashes as a bed? Will you call this a fast, even an acceptable day to the Lord? Is this not the fast which I choose, to loosen the bonds of wickedness, to undo the bands of the yoke, and to let the oppressed go free and break every yoke? Is it not to divide your bread with the hungry and bring the homeless poor into the house; when you see the naked, to cover him; and not to hide yourself from your own flesh? (Isaiah 58:5-7 NASB)

According to *Webster's Dictionary,* the word *breakthrough* means: "a sudden increase in knowledge, understanding, etc.; an important discovery that happens after trying for a long time to understand or explain something; a person's first important success; an offensive military assault that penetrates and carries beyond a defensive line; an act or instance of moving through or beyond an obstacle."

We must understand as Christian believers that our words carry life and death, blessings and curses, healing and sickness, poverty and prosperity, and liberty and bondage. As joint heirs with Christ it is the intention of the Lord to see you walk in totally liberty. It is the Father's heart to see you walk in peace, joy, and righteousness in the Holy Spirit each day of your life. You do not have to live under the curse of the law; you become justified by faith in Christ Jesus. You are not a curse but a blessing.

Breaking Curses

What is a curse? Why should you learn how to break curses, whether spoken in ignorance, anger, or through sin that has not been repented of? There are more things we must do than just speak decrees and declarations. We must make sure that we live our lives each day in alignment with the Holy Spirit so that we do not enslave ourselves by being outdated. At Calvary, Jesus broke the curse off our lives so that we can walk victorious in Him.

According to *Webster's Dictionary* the word *curse* means: "an offensive word that people say when they are angry; magical words that are said to cause trouble or bad luck for someone or the condition that results when such words are said." Furthermore, a *curse* is "a prayer or invocation for harm or injury; evil or misfortune that comes as if in response to imprecation or as retribution."

Jesus understood the effect of curses in a person's life. That is why in Luke 6:28 He says, *"Bless those who curse you, pray for those who mistreat you"* (NIV). Jesus knew how to reverse curses and bring about divine blessings upon those He interacted with. When a curse is broken and reversed, blessings are automatically released. In other words, Jesus was telling His disciples not to curse those who cursed them but to do the opposite by blessing those who curse you and being a blessing.

We must understand that the enemy cannot curse what God blesses. Even though there are word curses sent against us, we must be Christ-like and bless those who curse us. We can declare blessings over every word curse sent by the enemy. As kingdom believers we must empower ourselves daily by the Holy Spirit, who gives us wisdom and spirit-filled words that will encourage, build up, edify, console, and exhort.

That is why I love the prophetic ministry so much. The gift of prophecy is a building gift that encourages, edifies, and consoles a person (see John 4:16-19; 1 Cor. 14:1-12; Rom. 12:6). The words that we speak over others and ourselves should be filled with positivity and life. I am reminded what the Bible declares *"On the day of judgment people will give account for every careless word they speak"* (Matt. 12:36 ESV). It is God's desire that we become agents of blessing! We can break curses and release blessings. When the Lord created man in His image and according to His likeness, He blessed them, male and female, and said to them, *"Be fruitful and multiply, and fill the earth, and subdue it; and rule over…every living thing that moves on the earth"* (Gen. 1:28 NASB).

Releasing Blessings

We can see that Creator God's second blessing was upon man, and their blessing was connected to what He declared over them to do. After the Fall of Man, to be fruitful was a special blessing and to be unfruitful was a curse. There is a special, divine blessing that comes upon His people when they are fruitful, productive, reproduce themselves, fill the earth, place things under their feet, and rule and manage what God has given them charge over as His spiritual offspring. It has always been the Father's heart to see you successful and blessed in Jesus Christ. According to *Webster's Dictionary*, the word *bless* means "to make holy; to ask the favor or protection of God for; to confer prosperity or happiness upon." We can see that when we are blessed, we are to be happy, possess divine favor and endowment, and glorify God.

We must break through in the truth of God's Word and what He says about us. We must prophesy and speak the will of God over our lives to see prophetic breakthrough. When a Christian believer is blessed, they become blissful, beautified, joyful, peaceful, sacred in God's eyes. What are you framing daily through your words? What are you releasing over your own life, children, ministry, church, business, career, marriage, relationships, city, nation, and health? Are you speaking from God's perspective and viewpoint?

My heart is to see lovers of Christ walk in the power of the spoken word, receive total victory, and embrace their divine season of breakthrough. We do not have to live beneath our natural and spiritual means but live by the code of biblical principles that releases blessing and break curses. God is a covenantal God. Jesus has died for our sins so that we are back in right fellowship with the Father.

Being justified by faith, we are now joint heirs. Covenants are only established through mutual agreement. The most powerful vehicle in the earth is communication. Bad communication can break a great relationship and good communication can build a great relationship. Jesus desires for us to be blessed daily and live in a realm of divine access to those blessings through the law of obedience and walking in covenant relationship with Daddy God.

God is in the blessings and favor releasing business. There are those who oppose any teaching on blessings from God because they believe its leans toward prosperity Gospel. I guess they believe that the life of the believer is always to be boring, going through suffering, persecution, and betrayal. God is a loving Father. What father do you know who does not want to see his children succeed even in the midst of adversity? We are to be the head and not the tail, a lender and not a borrower, first and not last. Jesus became poor that we might become wealthy in Him. Do not believe any teaching that says that God does not want the best for His children.

God made man in His image and according to His likeness and created a place called Eden, which was a parkland of pleasure, enjoyment, fertility, fruitfulness, blessings, amusement, productivity, plenty, peace, joy, and righteousness where God's presence was there with Adam and Eve. God blessed it and called it very good in His sight. It is my heart that you see the good come out of your life and that the blessing of the Lord makes you rich and breaks every sorrow.

The Lord of the Breakthrough

Allow the Holy Spirit to give you words that are life-creating and life-changing and will bring you to a place of breakthrough. God wants to take you to a divine place prophetically as He did with King David. This places is called "Baal-perazim" which means the "Master Breaker, Lord of the Breakthrough, Lord of the Breaches and the Lord has broken through my enemies."

> *Then David inquired of the Lord, saying. "Shall I go up against the Philistines? Will You give them into my hand?" And the Lord said to David, "Go up, for I will certainly give the Philistines into your hand." So David came to Baal-perazim and defeated them there; and he said, "The Lord has broken through my enemies before me like the breakthrough of waters." Therefore he named that place Baal-perazim* (2 Samuel 5:19-20 NASB).

David inquired of the Lord after being anointed king over all of Israel and Judah. By evicting the Jebusites in the city of David, the Philistines heard that David was anointed king and they formed an army to defeat him. God gave a strategy to David after he sought the Lord's counsel and directives to defeat his enemies. God gave him clearance to move forward to fight. The Lord was with David and they defeated the front lines of the Philistines. Due to the flawless victory David called that place Baal-perazim, declaring that the Lord had broken through his enemies. David compared the enemies defeat through the power of God to the breaking through of many waters. There are places in our lives God wants to bring us to—places of breakthrough.

Heaven is pregnant with your purpose and destiny at the place called Baal-perazim. Heaven's water is breaking with the blessings and provisions of the Lord that will overtake, overshadow, and overwhelm you. The enemy will not cause your destiny and dream to be stillborn or aborted. Your dream will come full term in the spirit. The God of Heaven will remove every abortionist spiritually in your life who comes to withdraw and kill your divine assignment in the earth.

God Will Burst Through Your Enemies

When the heavens rend, break, or tear open over your life, get ready for the rain of blessing and the judgment against the enemies of God. In the New Living Translation, I like how David explained what God was doing: *"He burst through my enemies like a raging flood!"* I prophesy to you, the reader, that God will burst through like a raging flood against every spiritual enemy and demon and that in turn He will open the floodgates of Heaven's compensation and restitution as your just reward and judgment.

Whatever spiritual Philistine or giant you may be facing in your life that is causing personal defeat or failure, know that as you inquire of the Lord Jesus each day, the Lord will give you the instructions, wisdom, strategy, and empowerment of the Holy Spirit to be victorious and not victimized by the enemies of your past or present. As you seek the Lord daily, you will see the Lord of the breakthrough come in your life and bring flawless victories on your behalf. You will be like King David after your personal 90-day journey and see the supernatural favor and strength of your King give you spiritual breakthroughs that Heaven wants you to encounter. You will live each day in that place called Baal-perazim, where God has burst through on your behalf to bring your *Prophetic Breakthrough!*

Chapter Two

BREAKING CURSES TO RELEASE BLESSINGS

"Is not My word like fire?" declares the Lord,
"and like a hammer which shatters a rock?

—Jeremiah 23:29 NASB

In Western civilization, when it comes to the word *curse* it often means someone "swearing" at someone using foul language, profanity, or perhaps even blasphemous words against God. However, the biblical meaning of the word carries a greater weight in its usage than what we are accustomed to in our society or culture. Biblically, cursing is not only speaking evil against another party, but it is evil will, intention, and repercussions coming upon someone.

According to the Bible, if a person is under a curse or has been cursed, the notion is that evil has come upon them in some way, whether it is debt, illness, sickness, disease, pain, tragedy, or bad circumstances that manifest in that person's life as a result of the curse. Please note that not all personal issues, circumstances, or difficulties are due to a curse. I am not implying that, but I am speaking on the effects of curses generally.

Faith Test of Obedience

There are times when God leads the believer through faith testing circumstances to stretch their faith. God does this to help His people grow in grace and help them to mature in particular areas to grow stronger in their relationship with Him. God cursed satan for deceiving Eve, cursed creation itself for Adam's disobedience, and cursed Cain for his fratricide (see Gen. 3:14-17; 4:11). God takes His people through a process that leads them by His Spirit through situations and circumstances to mature them so that in turn they may experience His overcoming power and find His will and purpose for their lives.

Disobedience to the will and Word of God will bring curses upon a person. Obedience releases blessings, and disobedience can bring judgment. This chapter is speaking in reference to evil curses that come from evil agents, wicked men, and the enemy. Remember the definition of the word *curse?* "A prayer for harm to come upon one; something that is cursed; evil or misfortune." Let us look at the synonyms for the word *curse*—anathema, damnation, denunciation, hex, and spell.

Today in many cultures there are witches, warlocks, false prophets, witch doctors, or shamans that speak forth curses or false prophecies on people through demonic powers and spirits. Furthermore, there are charismatic believers who have been guilty of operating in charismatic witchcraft prayers, prophecies, and curses to control, manipulate, and dominate other believers. These are cases of *unknown witchcraft,* practiced in the Christian world by those in leadership positions. For example, a spiritual leader or pastor who tries to control those he or she leads is practicing witchcraft. He or she may feel they are acting in the best interests of those they are leading, but they have no authority to force their own will on others for personal gain or their own interests. In addition, using their spiritual gifts to control and influence a person's decision for their own gain instead of the glory of God is operating in charismatic witchcraft. Spiritual gifts are used to build, edify, and bless the believer, not to control them by influencing their personal will. This should not be so in the Body of Christ.

Invisible Barriers and Restrictions

Curses becomes invisible barriers and restrictions in the spirit. They are not discerned and detected with the natural eyes. It will take spiritual eyes and the gift of discerning of spirits to detect them. When a person speaks hateful words of destruction toward an individual, they become trajectory curses that are projected just as much as in voodoo with the stabbed doll. When word curses are sent, they are like daggers that bring harm, pain, and even death. The curses spoken over a voodoo doll do not come to pass because of the doll or the pins. There is no power in those inanimate objects. They happen because of the demonic power operating through the person speaking forth the curses. We have to understand that there is death and life in the power of our tongues (see Prov. 18:21). We have to be mindful and careful of what we speak forth out of our mouths—they carry creative or destructive powers and measures! They can carry great words of life or grave words of death. I am speaking spiritually here.

> Samuel said, "Has the Lord as much delight in burnt offerings and sacrifices as in obeying the voice of the Lord? Behold, to obey is better than sacrifice, and to heed than the fat of rams. For rebellion is as the sin of divination, and insubordination is as iniquity and idolatry. Because you have rejected the word of the Lord, He has also rejected you from being king" (1 Samuel 15:22-23 NASB).

We can see that as King Saul rejected the Word of the Lord, God rejected him as king. Saul technically cursed himself, and the scripture says that rebellion is witchcraft and disobedience is sin. We know that iniquity is the absence of moral or spiritual values, an unjust act, and morally objectionable behavior. Some Christian believers are not seeing prophetic breakthroughs, deliverance, freedom, healing, and liberty in their lives due to an act of disobedience to God's Word, will, and standard.

God wants to bring spiritual breakthrough by breaking curses that may be plaguing His people due to unrepentant sins committed against God knowingly or unknowingly. In many cultures outside of western societies, people have no problem understanding curses and blessings because the presence of demonic beings is very real to them. In fact, in many cultures plagued with sorcery and witchcraft people leave monetary offerings to appease demonic spirits so they will leave them alone. Curses are real and should not be ignored. God's people do not perish because of demons, poverty, debt, sickness, or disease but because of lack of knowledge and rejection of the truth (see Hos. 4:6).

Generational Curses and Strongholds

Have you ever seen a family in which the father had an issue with uncontrollable anger, and his son over time "inherited" it and the grandfather also had the same anger problem? Or have you noticed something about yourself that you desire to change and later found out that your mother and her father also suffer from that same issue as well? Many people in today's society are living under a spirit of bondage that the sins of their ancestors or forefathers have handed down to them unwillingly.

> *Keeping mercy for thousands, forgiving iniquity and transgression and sin, by no means clearing the guilty, visiting the iniquity [punishing] of the fathers upon the children and the children's children to the third and the fourth generation* (Exodus 34:7 NKJV).

> *Our fathers have sinned, and are not; and we have borne [been punished for] their iniquities* (Lamentations 5:7 KJV).

I believe some things become learned behaviors, and some things are in a person's DNA, inherited from their mother and father, whether negative or positive. I do not believe someone is born a racist but is raised with those types of discriminating values by those who are in authority over them. Just as I do not believe someone is born a homosexual, but they can be exposed to that type of lifestyle and culture. It is up to the individual to reject or embrace the belief that this is their own sexual orientation even though it violates biblical standards and moral values of God's Word.

Breaking Generational Strongholds

Generational curses are a spiritual bondage passed down from one generation to another. One of the symptoms of a generational curse is a perpetual negative pattern that has been passed down from generation to generation. Generational curses can be inherited or passed down genetically and spiritually. There are even those who are adopted and carry the same genetic characteristics, flaws, and negatives attributes of their birth parents.

Oddly, a person who is adopted may not be raised by their birth parents but can still pick up their natural parents' negative patterns of behavior. Why? Because at the end of the day, they inherited their spiritual bondage from their birth parents and not their adopted parents. For example, an African who was adopted and raised in a Chinese culture and family is still biologically African. They have similarities with their Chinese family because they are all human, but in their DNA there is a difference. The African will carry the physical traits and medical history of their birth parents even if they are adopted into another family. They have the DNA of their birth father and mother, not their adopted ones. They can learn and adapt to the Chinese culture, but at the end of the day their DNA is African.

Another type of generational curse is family sickness, hereditary diseasepoverty, mental dysfunction, and financial debt. There are spiritual bondages of diseases that are passed down from one generation to the next. We commonly see cancer—a physical manifestation of a spiritual bondage. Moreover, we can see mental disabilities, continual financial difficulties, phobias, ungodly fetishes, persistent irrational fears, paranoia, and depression. We have to understand that anything that becomes a persistent struggle or hardship passed down from one generation to the next may very well be a spiritual bondage.

God can break every stronghold in our lives. There is no curse, hex, spell, or enchantment that cannot be shattered by the power of God. You have been given authority by the Holy Spirit to exercise your spiritual dominion over any curses or generational strongholds sent by the enemy. As Christian believers, we have to know our spiritual rights and authority in God's Word. Did you know that ignorance could become a stronghold of deception that keeps us from receiving our spiritual breakthrough? The enemy comes to blind unbelievers to the truth, so how much more will he come to those who walk in the spirit of truth?

> *The god of this age has blinded the minds of unbelievers, so they cannot see the light of the gospel that displays the glory of Christ, who is the image of God. For what we preach is not ourselves, but Jesus Christ as Lord, and ourselves as your servants for Jesus' sake. For God, who said "Let light shine out of darkness," made his light shine in our hearts to give us the light of the knowledge of God's glory displayed in the face of Christ* (2 Corinthians 4:4-6 NIV).

The agenda of the enemy is to keep people from seeing the light and truth of God's Word. He would rather them stay in darkness (ignorance) than in the light (truth). As I stated before, lack of knowledge causes people to perish because of ignorance. We have to disarm the enemy by knowing how to break curses so that we can receive our spiritual inheritance and the divine blessings of the Lord in our lives. Curses hinder blessings from flowing in.

Purpose of Generational Curses

God was so disgusted with sin that He would punish future generations for the sins of their ancestors. One of the sentences by the Lord for someone found practicing witchcraft was the death penalty (see Exod. 22:18). Adam was the first who fell from glory and created a wave of generational curses to follow the next generation. The entire human race suffered due to one man's disobedience. God takes rebellion seriously, and the sins of the ancestors influence the following generations.

God knew that people's prized possessions were their children and children's children, and therefore it makes sin a lot harder to commit when you realize that you are not the only one who is being punished for it, but also your legacy will pay a dear price for your disobedience and rebellious decisions. I believe this is the reason and purpose behind generational curses. The first Adam fell because of disobedience, but God raised up the last Adam in Jesus who restored our place in right fellowship, in covenant with the Father through His obedience. Jesus is the curse breaker!

Jesus Is the Curse Breaker!

One of the ways that generational curses are broken is when one accepts Jesus as Lord over their life. The transference of spiritual bondage from your ancestors comes to a total halt. A newborn believer in Christ is no longer responsible and receives freedom from their ancestors' spiritual bondages once they accept Jesus! The transfer has been broken in Jesus' blood and at Calvary's cross. We as believers are liberated from the curse of sin, both our personal ones and those committed by our ancestors. I love what Galatians 3:13 says: *"Christ hath redeemed us from the curse of the law, being made a curse for us: for it is written, Cursed is every one that hangeth on a tree"* (KJV).

We must understand that once we are adopted in the Kingdom of God as a child of God, no longer will the sins of our forefathers bring upon us spiritual curses, strongholds, and bondages. God comes to break every chain of any generational curse. We are no longer accountable for what someone else committed.

> *In those days they shall say no more, The fathers have eaten a sour grape, and the children's teeth are set on edge. But every one shall die for his own iniquity: every man that eateth the sour grape, his teeth shall be set on edge* (Jeremiah 31:29-30 KJV).

So why are there so many believers who seem to be living under a generational curse? This puzzled me too before I understood how it works. There are bondages that were already passed down to a person before they came into covenant with God. The legal grounds are certainly paid for on the cross and therefore broken after salvation. The only thing left to do is cast out any spirits that have gained entrance before one has accepted Jesus Christ in their heart.

Entrance Way to Generational Curses

A generational curse is a spiritual stronghold that hinders spiritual breakthrough. It keeps a person from walking in their prophetic destiny in God. Curses can open doors in people's lives that give demons legal influence and access. If a person is involved in any type of sin or has opened a door out of ignorance—whether a person dabbled in the occult, magic, new age, palm or tarot card reading, psychic prediction, drugs, or sexual sins—then it is imperative to regain any legal ground (or stronghold) that gave the enemy legal right to create the spiritual bondage. For example, if a person has consulted a psychic, then they have just given legal right for demonic entities to enter and those spirits will bring about deception and curses (strongholds).

We must recall to memory when and how the door was opened and take back legal ground first, then cast out the spirits. Jesus understood this principle and how the satanic kingdom operates. He said, *"No man can enter into a strong man's house, and spoil his goods, except he will first bind the strong man; and then he will spoil his house"* (Mark 3:27 KJV). Jesus understood that satan is the strong man. To plunder and get legal ground in the hierarchy of satan's kingdom, you must first bind the strong man, then enter his house, and then you can plunder his goods. We must clearly know that wherever we have given up legal ground in our life, we must identify the strong man and bind him, then cast him out to release victory. We have to be gatekeepers and doorkeepers over our spiritual house—body and soul (mind, will, and emotions). Do not allow anything contrary to God's will and purpose to enter. Our bodies are the temple of the Holy Spirit (see 1 Cor. 6:19).

I truly believe that bitterness, unforgiveness, and resentment can open doorways for generational strongholds and ungodly soul ties. I have come across several believers who are suffering from cancer because of unforgiveness. Unforgiveness is a subtle spirit that eats away at a person and over time it serves as a blockage to blessing and even the forgiveness of your own sins (see Matt. 6:15).

Decree What's Rightfully Yours

Our words can bless us or even curse us. Take action today by dismantling any curses and generational strongholds that come in season to break your will. To receive prophetic breakthrough is to come into agreement with your destiny and fall out of agreement with what once was. Never think that the Lord does not respond on behalf of what you confess, decree, and release out of your mouth. Healing is in your mouth. Healing is linked to your confession and what you want to see happen. When you confess and repent, healing is released. God hears and responds to the prayer of confession made by the righteous.

Therefore, confess your sins to one another and pray for one another, that you may be healed. The prayer of a righteous person has great power as it is working (James 5:16 ESV).

Here is a great sample confession prayer you can use to do just that:

In the name of Jesus, I confess the sins and iniquities of my parents (name specific sins if known), grandparents (name specific sins if known), and all other ancestors. I declare that by the blood of Jesus these sins have been forgiven and satan and his demons can no longer use these sins as legal ground in my life! In the name of Jesus and by the power of His blood, I now declare that all generational curses have been renounced, broken, and severed, and I am no longer under their bondage! In the name of Jesus, I declare myself and my future generations loosed from any bondages passed down to me from my ancestors. Amen!

I do not believe Christians can live under generational curses and strongholds once they are saved. However, I do believe they can be impacted greatly by demonic influences that entered through generational curses before they gave their life to Jesus. Just like people whose past actions have caused them to experience oppression in their lives before they accepted Christ, they picked up demonic residue because of their past sin, which followed them after conversion. God forgives people of their sins at salvation, but the demons do not forget. That is why the spirits have to be bound and cast out. We must understand that the curses are broken at conversion, but that does not guarantee that demons automatically leave at salvation. Likewise, demons that enter in through generational curses have to be evicted and the door finally shut (curse broken).

Don't Curse Your Legacy

Generational curses have the power to affect generations to come, as we see in Genesis 9:24-25: "*And Noah awoke from his wine, and knew what his younger son had done unto him. And he said, Cursed be Canaan; a servant of servants shall he be unto his brethren"* (KJV). Noah was drunk and was not in the best condition when found by one of his sons, Ham. As a result, Ham saw his father's nakedness and exposed him to his other brothers. Instead of covering his father and concealing what he saw, he mocked him, which caused Noah to curse Ham and Ham's children. Noah carried so much authority that his words touched nations unborn. As you read Genesis 9, you will notice later on that Noah's curse ended up affecting an entire generation.

These types of generational curses are sent diabolically and can be renounced and broken by the power of God. The power that was used to create a curse will take the same counteractive power to break it. The power of the spoken word can break the strongholds of curses sent by hatred, jealousy, envy, murder, and division. As believers we should never be ignorant of the enemy's devices, including curses, and must educate ourselves on how they work. If you are unsure whether a curse has been broken, I suggest verbally breaking it anyway, just so you know for sure that it is broken for the last time. Here is a sample prayer you can declare aloud to break yourself free from any spoken generational curses and strongholds:

> *In the name of Jesus and by the power of His blood, I now renounce, break, and sever all curses that have been handed down to me from my ancestors. In the name of Jesus, I now loose myself and my future generations from any bondages passed down to me from my ancestors!*

These are the seven biblical keys to break curses and release blessings:

1. Prayer (Matt. 17:21; Mark 9:29)

2. Fasting (Isa. 58:6)

3. Repentance (Heb. 6:6)

4. Knowing the Scriptures and God's power (Matt. 22:29)

5. Worship (Ps. 111)

6. Praise and prayer (Acts 16:16-40)

7. Anointing that destroys yokes (Isa. 10:27)

Curses Can Work Against You

I believe wholeheartedly that in today's society, some Christian believers still contend against curses that are working against them. They may see tremendous breakthrough in some areas, but other areas are in constant warfare. It is not only demonic curses; there are also demonic agencies sent against ministry gifts to hinder, persecute, and stop forward advancement in God's kingdom. In various places around the world, there are open occult practices that target faith-based organizations and Christians. There are territorial spirits that are governing in regions blocking any opening for spiritual breakthrough.

Curses can work against us. That is why we must be careful what we speak, especially if we are not delivered from profanity. Profanity is sin and should not be used in the culture of the kingdom.

> *But now ye also put off all these; anger, wrath, malice, blasphemy, filthy communication out of your mouth. Lie not one to another; seeing that ye have put off the old man with his deeds; and have put on the new man, which is renewed in knowledge after the image of him that created him* (Colossians 3:8-10 KJV).

What we speak can be used against us, like the Miranda rights in the United States. When the police make an arrest, by protocol they are to read them their rights. They say that whatever one speaks can and will be used against them. As mature believers, we do not want the enemy to use ungodly or ignorant words that we speak against us to bring hindrance.

God is raising, equipping, and educating apostolic and prophetic ministries and churches in the area of spiritual warfare. Word curses and sorcery can greatly influence a believer who is called to do a mighty work for the Lord. God is raising up believers who will be able to detect and discern demonic intrusion and confront it head on. Believers must go in prayer and fasting and ask the Father to show them curses spoken against them before they gave their lives to Jesus or spiritual strongholds that have come upon them through involvement in witchcraft, iniquity, and idolatry (see Deut. 29:24-28).

As you know, you have been redeemed from the curse of the law through Christ, but if there is any act of premeditated rebellion or willful sin it will cause you to be a "covenant breaker," which will leave holes in your spiritual armor that will give the enemy access to bring curses on you. There are those out there who believe that the enemy cannot touch them or have access to them. This theory or doctrine is not truly supported by the Word of God.

The apostle wrote to the church of Ephesians not to give the devil any foothold or place (see Eph. 4:27). We must know that Paul was not speaking to unbelievers; he was writing to believers. I believe that curses work against believers if they are in active sin, open or secret rebellion to God's Word, or out of the divine purpose of God. However, if the believer is walking in God's will, in love, and in faith, then they will begin to see the release of God's divine blessings and witness curses broken through the act and law of obedience.

Jesus Took Away the Curse of the Law

Jesus took away the curse of the law when we accepted Him into our hearts. Before that, the law of sin and death bound us; but after we are regenerated by the Holy Spirit, we are now subject to the law of life in Christ Jesus, who became a curse for us. We now have access to all spiritual blessings. When a curse is broken off a person's life, they can walk in total freedom and deliverance in that area. They will begin to see that the blessing of the Lord makes them rich and adds no more sorrow.

> *For the law of the Spirit of life in Christ Jesus hath made me free from the law of sin and death* (Romans 8:2 KJV).

> *Christ hath redeemed us from the curse of the law, being made a curse for us: for it is written, Cursed is every one that hangeth on a tree: that the blessing of Abraham might come on the Gentiles through Jesus Christ; that we might receive the promise of the Spirit through faith* (Galatians 3:13-14 KJV).

Prayer That Breaks Curses and Releases Divine Blessings

The way to break a curse is to repent for whatever involvement has occurred on the enemy's territory and rebuke the devil out of your life. You should also pray something along the following lines:

Father, I ask You first to forgive me for my sins and cleanse me from any area where I have allowed the devil to enter my life. I renounce any involvement with the works of darkness. In the name of Jesus, I now cancel every curse and, Father, I ask You to forgive the people who have spoken them against me. I thank You that those curses will no longer operate against me. In Jesus' name, they are broken right now by the power of Almighty God. I cancel every evil that was spoken against me and ask You to cover me and my family with Your protection according to Your Word in Psalm 91. Now, Father, I ask that You release my spiritual inheritance. It is Your desire to give me the kingdom, and, because the kingdom is my first priority, loose what is mine rightfully. Father, I ask that You bless everything that I put my hands to do and release all spiritual blessings that You have for me and those connected to me. I am Your child and I am the head and not the tail, first and not last, and blessed and not cursed. Finally, Father, I can do all things through Christ who strengthens me, in Jesus' name.

The Bible tells us in James 4:7 to *"Submit yourselves therefore to God. Resist the devil, and he will flee from you."* Most people desire to see tremendous breakthroughs in their lives, especially when it comes to personal deliverance. I have seen people come to the altar to receive their deliverance, but after deliverance where was the follow-up or follow-through by the leadership of that church? I always make it my point to follow up with individuals who receive their breakthrough and deliverance. Most churches and leadership must understand the importance of this principle so that we will not lose the one seeking breakthrough. It is checks and balances to make sure that the individual maintains their freedom, deliverance, and breakthrough.

One principle that most people overlook when it comes to breakthrough and deliverance is that we must first submit to God. Once we submit totally to God, we can see that we have the power to resist the devil and he will flee. God wants to break any curses and ungodly soul ties. Soul ties I will talk about in Chapter Four: Breaking Ungodly Soul Ties. As we submit to God's will for our lives, curses and soul ties will not seek to affect us.

There was a time when I had individuals verbally curse my ministry and my life to my face, but I understood that it was not them speaking but the spirit behind the words. We are commanded by the Word of God to bless those who curse us. As believers, we should not send word curses back to the person sending the word curses. We must know that we are not fighting against the person but spiritual wickedness. We are not to return evil for evil, but rather overcome evil with good (see Rom. 12:21). We are to pray for them and ask the

Lord to forgive them because many times they do not know what they are doing and saying.

If you intercede for such persons, you are obeying the Word, which allows the Holy Spirit to cancel the curse automatically if you are speaking good and praying for those who would seek to harm you. You should also quote the Scriptures that promise protection, such as Psalm 91. I always send the words back to the enemy and not the person, and I pronounce sevenfold blessings over the word curses that was sent to manifest in my life immediately as a prophetic sign. What the enemy meant for my harm, God will reverse it for my good.

Chapter Three

WAGING PROPHETIC WARFARE

*This command I entrust to you, Timothy, my son,
in accordance with the prophecies previously made
concerning you, that by them you fight the good fight.*

—1 Timothy 1:18 NASB

The enemy does not know the mind, purpose, and things of God when it comes to your destiny. There is no special intelligence that the enemy receives from another source about you. I believe there are angels that are assigned to each person at birth and throughout their life. However, the enemy is a counterfeit and tries to duplicate the Kingdom of God, so likewise there are demons that are assigned as well to a person to monitor them. We know that the adversary is like a roaring lion and is not everywhere at the same time.

> *Cast all your anxiety on him because he cares for you.
> Be alert and of sober mind. Your enemy the devil prowls
> around like a roaring lion looking for someone to devour.
> Resist him, standing firm in the faith, because you know
> that the family of believers throughout the world is under-
> going the same kind of sufferings* (1 Peter 5:7-9 NIV).

The enemy does not have insight into the prophetic promises of God over your life. He is not God, who is omnipresent—everywhere at the same time. Demons are not everywhere at the same time and are not as numerous as the host of Heaven. A small portion of former angels, now called demons, were evicted out of Heaven. The enemy only receives knowledge of God's promises, will, original intent, and heart concerning you when it is prophesied, uttered, and released by God and His holy prophets. When true prophetic words are released over your life and the dreams of God are spoken forth verbally, the enemy has access and insight into what God desires to do in your life. His assignment is to keep you from ever walking into your destiny. He will put up a fight once the prophetic word is released.

Hell Unleashed after Prophecy Is Released

Have you received a word of prophecy or prophetic dream or vision from God and right after all hell is unleashed? Have you felt like you shared something personal that God revealed to you and were later met with some resistance? It is because of your prophecy! Joseph made the mistake of sharing his prophetic dream with his brothers and father, which caused unnecessary family drama, jealousy, and hatred. When there is a true prophecy spoken, it will initiate warfare. In other words, the spoken promises of God incite opposing or counteractive warfare.

I believe that when a true prophecy from God is released, all of hell gets nervous. There were prophetic words released before you were born. Jesus Himself faced constant satanic resistance and temptation before He was born, during His ministry, and at the cross until death. Herod got word of the prophecy of a coming Ruler, Governor and King of the Jews who would govern God's people. He became furious in his heart and sent out an assassination decree to put to death all the young males under two years old. Herod was terrified by the prophecy of Jesus.

Can you imagine what your personal prophecy and natural birthing did to the kingdom of darkness? Jesus' prophecy and birth triggered demonic warfare and resistance. I will go so far as to say that when a person gives their life over to Jesus and is born again, it also triggers warfare. I will not say that once a person is saved all their trouble will be over. However, I do know that if God is before you, then who can be against you? The Lord will protect His own and give them strategic plans to defeat the enemy's tactics. I can recall many times in the past when I would receive powerful prophetic words from prophetic leaders, and right after receiving that word I would find myself in an argument with a family member or co-worker or something would happen to me physically—I would get sick or take a financial hit. It was constant resistance, and I never could make sense of it until God revealed it to me in prayer while fasting. God reminded me of the parable of the seeds sown in the kingdom:

> *But blessed are your eyes because they see, and your ears because they hear. For truly I tell you, many prophets and righteous people longed to see what you see but did not see it, and to hear what you hear but did not hear it. Listen then to what the parable of the sower means: When anyone hears the message about the kingdom and does not understand it, the evil one comes and snatches away what was sown in their heart. This is the seed sown along the path* (Matthew 13:16-19 NIV).

Without Prophecy and Prophetic Vision

God revealed to me an application of Matthew 13 to prophetic words (seeds) that are sown (spoken) into our lives (hearts). The evil one comes to snatch away what was prophesied. The prophetic word serves as a pathway to our destiny. If the enemy can steal, kill, and destroy God's prophetic word over us than we will never see the spiritual and prophetic breakthrough in our lives. We will run around in circles in life trying to find our way. God's desire is to allow us to break through any barriers of resistance that the enemy brings our way. I had to learn the enemy's tactics in prayer and in the Word to outmaneuver him.

The enemy wants us ignorant of the purposes of God in our lives. If he can keep God's people blinded to their identity, calling, gifting, purpose, and destiny, then he has the upper hand. God will not have His people ignorant of the enemy's devices. We disarm him by fighting back with warfare strategies that will overcome the plans of the enemy.

> *Where there is no prophetic vision the people cast off restraint, but blessed is he who keeps the law* (Proverbs 29:18 ESV).

Without prophecy, divine guidance, revelation, and prophetic vision released by Heaven over our lives, the Bible says that people are unrestrained, made naked, unashamed, and undisciplined. Prophecy is God's idea and vehicle to release His original plan, intent, and purpose to be fulfilled in your life. Prophecy is important because God does not waste His breath. His words serve a divine and eternal purpose. The devil is already a defeated foe, but he will put up a fight to slow you down, stop you, and knock you out of the game. This is the time to beat him at his own game. This is more than just a game the enemy is playing. This is what I call "blood sport." It's a battle of the fittest, and only the strong will survive. We must wage war on the enemy. The rules of engagement are changing. We must engage first before he engages. It is a spiritual fight.

We are admonished in God's Word to *"put on the full armor of God, so that you can take your stand against the devil's schemes"* (Eph. 6:11 NIV). You must stand your ground and resist the resister. I like what 1 Peter 5:9 declares: *"Resist him, standing firm in the faith, because you know that the family of believers throughout the world is undergoing the same kind of sufferings"* (NIV). Suffering will come, but know that you have been given authority in Christ as you submit humbly the Lord to resist the enemy and he will flee. I am a huge fan of pressing into the Holy Spirit to receive my new battle plans. The enemy will find opportune times and seasons of vulnerability to wear out the saints of the kingdom. I believe it is time to put on our prophetic armor to wage war on the enemy.

Execute Prophetic Strategy for Breakthrough

To take back what belongs to us, we must mark the territory and draw a line in the sand with prayer. God will give His people a strategy and new rules of engagement as we inquire of the Lord. Joshua could not conquer Jericho without a victory plan. He marched the Israelites around the city once a day for six days, then seven times on the seventh day. The priests blew the trumpets and sent out a battle cry on the last blast (see Josh. 6). This conquering strategy was for Jericho, but that does not mean that the same war strategy would work for every single battle. We must discern, detect, and examine by the Holy Spirit what war plan works for each battle.

The enemy is a master war strategist, and we must inquire of God to execute and carry out effectively what He desires for us to do. There are different types of battles that we have to discern. We demolish arguments and every pretension that sets itself up against the knowledge of God, and we take captive every thought to make it obedient to Christ (see 2 Cor. 10:5). I believe we are held responsible in wage prophetic warfare. In other words, we have to prophesy and contend over the prophecies that has gone before us.

When I was ordained and set apostolically as a prophet in the Body of Christ in my local church, several months after the ordination I went through intense warfare. I knew that it was because of the charge, prophecy and commission that was released over me by the laying on of hands that imparted more spiritual gifts. Instantly, I discerned that what was released and ordained in Heaven was now established on earth, and the enemy was not happy about it. The enemy tried many times to shut my mouth as a young prophet. He did not want me to speak, preach, and declare what Heaven was saying and doing in my generation.

In the Word of God, the apostle Paul charged his spiritual son Timothy through the prophetic presbytery: *"This command I entrust to you, Timothy, my son, in accordance with the prophecies previously made concerning you, that by them you fight the good fight"* (1 Tim. 1:18 NASB). There is power in prophecy and impartation. The apostle Paul understood the significance of it, and he included it in his prophetic commendation and admonishment. *The Message Bible* says prophecies should make you *"fearless in your struggle, keeping a firm grip on your faith and on yourself. After all, this is a fight we're in."*

The Amplified Bible, Classic Edition translation goes on to encourage us to be *"inspired and aided"* by the prophetic words so that *"you may wage the good warfare."* The New Living Translation puts it like this: the prophetic words of release will *"help you fight well in the Lord's battles."* In other words, your prophetic word will fight for you and protect you. There is no doubt about it—we are in a fight indeed, but know that it is a good fight of faith against invisible enemies. Our spiritual battles are not with each other in the Body of Christ but with doctrines of men, doctrines of devils, generational curses passed down, spiritual strongholds, debt, sickness, disease, and the spirits that bring them.

Weapon of Prophecy

> *For our struggle is not against flesh and blood, but against the rulers, against the authorities, against the powers of this dark world and against the spiritual forces of evil in the heavenly realms* (Ephesians 6:12 NIV).

We can see from the above passage of Scripture that our warfare is not against each other. We are not called to dominate each other in Christ's kingdom. The warfare is against your prophetic word. The Word of the Lord spoken over you is what the enemy is after.

If the enemy can wear you out, drain, and deplete you then he can overtake you. One of Jesus' purposes in being sent to the earth was to destroy the works of satan. Jesus understood that His meat (nourishment) was doing what the Father sent Him to do. That should be the same mentality and mandate for Christian believers. Our spiritual diet, appetite, and cravings are fulfilling what we were born to do.

Jesus suffered much and paid a dear price on the cross for *you* to have eternal life. Warfare is inevitable as a believer. Daniel understood this every time he prayed. There was a time when Daniel prayed, and an angel told him that from the first day he started praying God heard his words and the angel came because of his words. There are spiritual weapons that are likened to natural ones, but the ones that believers use and engage with are not natural or physical but spiritual weapons.

Spiritual Weapons of Mass Destruction

For though we walk in the flesh, we do not war after the flesh: (for the weapons of our warfare are not carnal, but mighty through God to the pulling down of strong holds); *casting down imaginations, and every high thing that exalteth itself against the knowledge of God, and bringing into captivity every thought to the obedience of Christ; and having in a readiness to revenge all disobedience, when your obedience is fulfilled* (2 Corinthians 10:3-6 KJV).

In the above Scripture, the apostle Paul is defending his apostleship and speaking to an audience that may have had some doubts about his doctrine and position as an apostle. He says the weapons of our warfare are not carnal and later goes on to explain where the power abides—in God. This is not a natural or carnal battle but a spiritual one that needs only God's intervention to win.

We must understand that to be a believer is to engage in warfare. That's the price! Paul is reminding the people that there is a war going on. It is a spiritual war, and it has to be engaged spiritually and not carnally. One cannot win spiritual battles with physical or carnal weapons. It will take God's help and empowerment to win.

When the apostle Paul charged his spiritual son Timothy at ordination, he admonished him by prophetically speaking: *"This charge I commit unto thee, son Timothy...that thou by them mightest war a good warfare"* (1 Tim. 1:18 KJV). He was saying to him, "Son, you are in a battle, in warfare, and it is not going to be a walk in the park." Furthermore, we can see that Timothy was the same person to whom the apostle Paul wrote, encouraging him apostolically as a spiritual father, *"Endure hardness, as a good soldier of Jesus Christ"* (2 Tim. 2:3 KJV). We can see that we are called *good soldiers*. We are not called "chocolate soldiers" who melt under pressure but real soldiers who carry heavy machinery to fight.

Many Christian believers today do not realize that they are in spiritual warfare. There is a constant beating they encounter daily, weekly, monthly, or even in reoccurring cycles annually. They find themselves saying, "There is always something happening—it's one thing after another." I know I have found myself saying this. There will be conflict. Many of the Lord's people do not know that they are in spiritual combat. They are feeling the punches from the enemy but are not aware that they are in a heavy weight battle of their life. They only feel spiritually the impact of the fight, and by that time it is too late.

Fighting a Good Fight

If there is warfare going on in your life, you must know that the Bible says, *"There was war in heaven"* according to Revelation 12:7. Oftentimes our view of Heaven is a place of peace, joy, and happiness. That is true, but God talks about a war also going on there. While on earth, believers are going to be engaged in some level of warfare throughout their Christian walk. The apostle Paul was prophetically sensitive and discerning what was going on spiritually, and he was always conscious of this spiritual warfare against his life, calling, and apostolic ministry. We can understand with certainty why he said at the end of his life's journey, *"I have fought a good fight, I have finished my course, I have kept the faith"* (2 Tim. 4:7 KJV). What are we to do as soldiers? We are to do what any soldier would do: *"Put on the whole armour of God"* (Eph. 6:11 KJV).

This is a war cry summoning and rallying every believer—not some, but all—to *put on the armor of God.* This spiritual armor contends in a spiritual battle that needs spiritual weapons and spiritual wisdom and strategy to win it. This is how we are going to see prophetic and spiritual breakthrough in every area of our lives. *"Put on the whole armor of God, that ye may be able to stand against the wiles of the devil"* (Eph. 6:11 KJV). Spiritual armor and weapons are strongholds against the wiles of the devil. You cannot experience tremendous spiritual breakthrough without fighting and winning spiritual battles. Your prophetic destiny is at stake.

You may be asking what we are wrestling against. Let us look at them in verse 12: *"For we wrestle not against flesh and blood, but against principalities, against powers, against the rulers of the darkness of this world, against spiritual wickedness in high places"* (KJV).

1. Principalities

2. Powers

3. Rulers of darkness

4. Spiritual wickedness in high places

We can see that it is not a flesh and blood (carnal) battle but a spiritual one that demonically influences people, systems, government, leaders, and spiritual wickedness in the heavenlies and those who are in seats of power and authority (see Eph. 6:12). This is not warfare against your brother and sister in Christ or other people but against spirits. You have to realize how powerful you are in Christ. You are a lethal threat to the kingdom of darkness. The constant battle you are facing daily is against real demons and supernatural forces. Do you feel that conflict? Do you realize you are in a spiritual conflict? Do you realize how important you are? God is going to use you as tool in His hand to combat the enemy in the earth.

Spiritual Resistance against Your Destiny

Daniel the prophet understood that demonic forces were operative in the second heaven, resisting the prayer decrees released. There were influential territorial spirits operative under the empire of the king of Persia. Whoever is in authority opens the door and gives legal access to those types of demonic entities. Daniel's mantle and anointing in the realm of the spirit was ranked high, and he carried governmental spiritual authority as a prophet. When Daniel prayed, it shook things in the spiritual until eventually he created a stir of controversy and they wanted to silence him and change laws against the Jews. Moreover, there was a time when Daniel prayed and met conflict, and this was God's response to him through the archangel Gabriel:

> For from the first day that you set your heart on understanding this and on humbling yourself before your God, your words were heard, and I have come in response to your words. But the prince of the kingdom of Persia was withstanding me for twenty-one days; then behold, Michael, one of the chief princes, came to help me, for I had been left there with the kings of Persia (Daniel 10:12-13 NASB).

We can see that when a believer prays the enemy will send an assault to hinder breakthrough in the area that you have been praying, decreeing, and believing God for. Do not give up! Breakthrough only comes when you are consistent and persistent. Daniel did not allow demonic legislation and edicts to change his posture of prayer, and he saw prophetic words come through to bless God's people. I want you to understand how important it is to war over your prophecy and see prophetic breakthrough happen not only for you but also for your church, family, city, business, children, marriage, health, finances, ministry, community, life, and legacy. The deceiving tactics of the devil is to slow your forward progress and momentum.

The Enemy Will Change Times and Laws

He will speak out against the Most High and wear down the saints of the Highest One, and he will intend to make alterations in times and in law; and they will be given into his hand for a time, times, and half a time. But the court will sit for judgment, and his dominion will be taken away, annihilated and destroyed forever (Daniel 7:25-26 NASB).

I want you to notice something that stood out to me in the above text—the adversary will wear down the saints of the Most High, *"and he will intend to make alterations in times and in law."* We are seeing this type of agenda politically and in natural civil government. There are demonic influences engaging in high seats of authority, and the church must not be political but *prophetic*. We must declare and prophesy the heart, will, and counsel of God that will influence the seven mountains of society. The policies, procedures, and agendas of the kingdom supersedes human governments, systems, and policies.

We learned from the above Scriptures that it is the intention of the enemy to wear you down and change times and laws to bind you. Daniel's prayer decrees and revelation broke through after 21 days. You will learn in the next chapter 21 ways to obtain prophetic breakthrough spiritually. Daniel understood the power of prayer and prophetic decrees that released his breakthrough answers. We can see angels were involved in spiritual warfare and in Daniel's prayer petition. Angels play an intriguing part in assisting the believers to receive their breakthrough. When there is a true Word of God released over your life, you must be alert in the spirit to be able to face some resistance against that prophecy. You need to do more than just receive a prophetic word or dream from the Lord and think that is it.

Angelic Reinforcement

Angels are sent to marshal and protect you. The warfare may intensify, but the victory and reward is greater. If there is war in Heaven, then God's special armed forces called angels are still warring in the heavenlies. God can dispatch them. Even Jesus stated that He could pray and summon 12 legions (that is, about 72,000 angels) to deliver Him (see Matt. 26:53). We can see in the Book of Exodus where the Lord to Moses that He would an angelic forces to go before him to drive the enemies out of the land (see Exod. 23:23).

Angels do not only respond the *voice* of the Lord but also to the written Word (*logos*) and the prophetic word of God (*rhema*) that is spoken by prophets and prophetic people. One principle I saw that gave Daniel, Jesus, and Paul the prophetic advantage in seeing breakthrough when wielding the weapons that are mighty through God is that they prayed and decreed them through adversity. If we decree them through, declare them through, pray them through, and prophesy them through, then we will see the prophetic promises of God's Word break through.

Finally, keep in mind what Paul said: *"I have fought a good fight, I have finished my course, I have kept the faith"* (2 Tim. 4:7 KJV). The apostle Paul was saying that it was all worth it, and we as believers are also fighting a good fight of faith more than we're fighting any demon or enemy of God.

Battle-axe of God's Word to Defeat the Enemy

We are fighting against a real enemy, but the battle is often the battle to trust and believe in your prophetic word. God's Word is true in the face of contrary situations that may abruptly interrupt our lives. We do not allow circumstances and situations to control and dominate our lives, but we are called to control and dominate circumstances and situations. Use the sword of the Spirit to defeat the enemy. God is going to use you as a spiritual battle-axe to defeat the adversary spiritually not carnally.

His Word is the final authority that we can trust and believe. I believe the time is now go back and listen to those prophetic words, dreams you journaled, and visions of God burning in your heart. Review those prophetic words, pray them through, and decree them forth by rising up against the enemy that is standing in the way of you receiving your prophetic breakthrough and reaching your God-ordained destiny. In Part Two of this book there are prophetic word activations, a prayer starter, decrees, and declarations to disarm the enemy. These decrees will break curses and release the blessings of God in your life. You will begin to apply pressure on the enemy's camp to relinquish what is yours. You will bind the strong man and take your spoils back. Your breakthrough is here and now!

Chapter Four

BREAKING UNGODLY SOUL TIES

*Be ye not unequally yoked together with unbelievers: for
what fellowship hath righteousness with unrighteousness?
and what communion hath light with darkness?*

—2 Corinthians 6:14 KJV

What are soul ties? Many times, we hear terms but do not understand of them. In this chapter, I want to briefly define soul ties and discuss whether they are biblical. Anyone first hearing this term would probably assume that a soul tie is something that is connected to the soul and that the function is just that—a soul connection. Well, that is correct—a soul tie is a soul connection.

A spiritual soul tie is the joining or knitting together of two people with the same purpose or heart. There are godly, healthy, and covenant soul ties such as marriage, business partners, church/ministry relationships, family, or comrades (friendships). However, there are also ungodly, unhealthy, and negative soul ties, which are relationships that bring a person into bondage, robbing a person of their will and bringing harm, emotional damage, and pain.

Are Soul Ties Biblical or Not?

Whether a person is a Christian believer or not, they can be involved in unhealthy relationships and establish soul (mind, will, and emotional) ties connected to past relationships. Any past relationships that went sour can create inner resentment, pain, bitterness, unforgiveness, fear, harm, and a cycle of issues emotionally. I come to declare that there is good news—if a person acknowledges that they are in bondage, then Jesus can set them free!

The term *soul ties* may not be taught in many religious circles. The specific words are not found in the Bible, but the function of their existence is. There are many terms that we hear that are not found in Scripture, such as:

- Rapture
- Easter
- Trinity
- Accept Jesus as your personal Savior
- Sinner's prayer
- Altar call
- Vacation Bible School
- Sunday school

Just because the term is not found specifically in the Bible does not mean the function is not found in the Scriptures. The word *soul* is found throughout the Scriptures. We know that the soul is the seat of our mind, will, and emotions. The soul is different from the spirit and body. We know that the human is made up of three dimensions—spirit, soul, and body. There are people who mix the soul and spirit up or think that they are the same in function. We will explore what creates a soul tie, whether soul ties are demonic or divine, whether soul ties can be broken, and the biblical examples of a soul tie. The enemy is after our soul, and if he can get our soul then he has our mind, will, and emotions. God desires that we be in good health and that our soul will prosper. There are healthy soul ties that are created and there are unhealthy ones.

Prosperity and blessings are linked to what is in our soul. I love what Dr. Cindy Trimm shared one time in a meeting that I attended when she talked about a "soul fast." In other words, detoxing ourselves of what we have been feeding our soul appetites. She said oftentimes "it's not what we are eating that creates buildup in our souls, but it's what's eating us." I want to put this in proper perspective as it relates to our relationships.

Covenant relationships that are established by God will bring great success, blessing, health, protection, and advancement in the area that you are called to. However, there are toxic ones that do the opposite, and we have to make sure that they do not plague our lives. There are soul ties that we may have established verbally, contractually, knowingly, or unknowingly. They can be hindering you from receiving all that God has for you and you do not even know it. Soul ties are easy to establish but often very hard to break, depending on the degree and time of the relationship.

Ungodly Soul Ties Can Be Broken

God wants us to remove any and every ungodly, unproductive, unfruitful, unhealthy, and unreliable soul tie that is keeping you from walking in your prophetic breakthrough. I felt that this topic was necessary because I receive many letters, emails, and messages from people who are having martial, relational, financial, health, and ministry problems and did everything they could possibly do and still no breakthrough. Soul ties are connected to a person until they themselves acknowledges it exist in their life, then break them or have someone with spiritual authority help them. I liken a soul tie to a string that over time becomes a thick rope, tough to break.

As I began to inquire of the Lord prophetically, He began to reveal to me past relationships I was involved in that needed to be broken with regard to the soul ties. He would reveal to me names of people and old verbal promises that I did not keep. God wanted me to address, break, and release the obligations. God would direct me in prayer how break and sever those soul links from past hurts, release old traumas, break past employment obligations, sexual encounters, verbal and contractual agreements, fellowships, and old alliances to past ministries and churches that brought about church hurt. God was detoxing my soul and giving me the prophetic edge and intelligence to get my life back on track. We have to learn how to combat for our soul.

Take Back Your Spiritual Residence

Moreover, I liken a soul tie to a bird's nest. When the bird builds their nest in a specific location, it creates a home but also a place of birthing. As the bird continues to mark that place as home, it becomes legal. I recall a time when in front of my house was a large bush and the birds would migrate to it all the time. One day I heard bird sounds in the morning, and it was a nest full of baby birds. I was not going to destroy the nest because of the eggs and the baby birds in it; that is, until I would go to work and the mother and father birds started swooping down to attack me and poke me with their beaks. It would happen every day in the morning going to work and at night coming home from work. Finally, enough was enough—I was not going to allow these territorial birds to take over my residence. They were not going to run me off, even though they were only protecting their young. It made sense, and God was giving me an image of soul ties and relationships. Whether good or bad, they are meant to be protected and guarded. That is why we in the Body of Christ need godly, pure, holy, healthy, integral, transparent, and truthful covenant soul ties and relationships.

I removed the birds' nest and the eggs, which was hard to do. The Lord spoke to me and said this is what usually happens when a soul tie is created. Over time, soul ties are hard to remove, break, and address because of the time that it held residence in our subconscious. We have to remove the seats and thrones in our souls that were not established by God and replace them with the seat of Christ in our heart, mind, and soul (seat of decisions). He is the

King over our lives and over our decisions, and we have to yield them to the Holy Spirit.

God desires to take total residence in His people. There are those who are plagued by past hurts, emotional trauma, physical illness, disease, and sexually transmitted spirits established by an open door and entrance through the power of agreement. The power of agreement to that which is profane, ungodly, and carnal will become the seat of sin, iniquity, or even satan and his demons. We have to guard not only our mouths but also our hearts.

Remove the Residue

When I removed the nest, there was a peace and joy because I did not have to worry about noise at night and being attacked by a swarm of black birds. Interestingly, a month later there was another nest, but this time there were two of them. I said to myself, *I am certain that I removed it all, and now there are two.* I could not believe it, and God spoke to me and said, "Hakeem, you may have removed the nest, but you have not removed the residue."

I asked the Lord, "Residue?"

He said, "Yes, you may have removed the temporary residence of the birds' nest, but you have not removed their permanent marking of the location (residue)." Therefore, because I did not remove the residue, which is the location, the birds were able to detect the spot and rebuild their nests—more and faster.

As Christian believers, we not only remove spirits and cut illegal soul ties but have to remove any and all marked spots of residue (legal rights and soul agreements) that are left behind. It is like a dog vomiting and returning to it and thinking it's a meal—disgusting, right? Or its like a dog urinating to mark a spot and it dries but never was the stain and scent ever washed away permanently. However, that is the reality of what is in people's souls. I am reminded of a reality television show on A&E called *Hoarders* that showed people who went through trauma and became hoarders. Their homes were cluttered with old junk that took up space. The problem is that these people with these symptoms have a hard time letting things go and coping with the reality that they have a problem. They do not believe that hoarding is a mental disease, and they are so afraid to throw away the old.

I believe this is the time to break the lie, denial, pride, and insanity and de-junk whatever has created unproductivity in our lives. God wants us totally free and whole again. With the bird nest, I had to remove the nest and also destroy the residue that was left behind by cutting the branches so that they could not rebuild in that place again. I had to do this several times until the birds got the point. I had to take back my home from predators, trespassers, and territorial birds!

I believe prophetically God wants the same thing for His people. Souls that are not healthy becomes like that birds' nest. We have to address them, combat them, remove them, and continue repeatedly until we see total freedom in our lives. There are godly soul ties that the Father wants His people to establish. I am reminded of the three-fold cord in the Bible, which is not easily broken (see Eccl. 4:12).

What Is the Soul?

One can examine a healthy or unhealthy relationship by the fruit that it bears—just like a good tree cannot bear bad fruit and vice versa. We have to inspect, investigate, and examine our relationships, partnerships, and alliances, making clear assessments of their results and being honest enough to boldly remove dead fruit and withered leaves. We have to examine what negative or positive impact people, places, and things have on our decisions. There is a soul war over your mind, will, and emotions. The soul war is over your prophetic destiny and word over your life. It is over your spiritual inheritance and eternal place with God.

What is the soul? According to *Webster's New World Dictionary*, the word *soul* means, "an entity which is regarded as being the immortal or spiritual part of a person and which, having no physical or material reality; the moral or emotional nature of a human being; vital or essential part." Christian believers must first understand what the *soul* is biblically. It is a transliterated Hebrew word—*nephesh*—meaning "soul, self, life, creature, person, appetite, mind, living being, desire, emotion, and passion" (Strong, H5315). The soul becomes the seat of appetites, emotions, passions, and activity of the mind, will, character, and the man himself or the individual.

Prophets Verses Psychics

The Greek word for "soul" is *psyche*—the seat of the feelings, desires, affections, and aversions (Strong, G590). When you look at the Greek word *psyche,* we can see why "psychics" are those who operate in the realm of the soul. They get their information from the familiar place of the soul and not from divine revelation. Psychics play on the soul and are not prophetic. Prophets do not operate by the soulish realm but by divine revelation, insight, wisdom, knowledge, and the counsel of God. Prophets speak by the Spirit of God to a person's spirit, and a psychic speaks by a familiar spirit by way of one's soul.

The word for "spirit" is a Greek word *pneuma,* which refers to the third person of the triune God, the Holy Spirit, coequal, coeternal with the Father and the Son (Strong, G4151). It means the personality and character (the "Holy" Spirit) and a life-giving spirit and sometimes emphasizes his work and power (the Spirit of Truth).

So let us explore briefly what the Bible says about soul ties, and then I will give you a soul tie-breaker for you to use in your prayer time with God. What is a soul tie? A soul tie is a real bond, connection, and tying of one relationship to another.

All the believers were one in heart and mind. No one claimed that any of their possessions was their own, but they shared everything they had (Acts 4:32 NIV).

Fulfill ye my joy, that ye be likeminded, having the same love, being of one accord, of one mind (Philippians 2:2 KJV).

For I have no man likeminded, who will naturally care for your state (Philippians 2:20 KJV).

We see the apostle Paul admonishing and reminding the Philippian church to be "likeminded." In the Greek this term is *isopsychos*, which means to be "equal in soul" (Strong, G2473). My point is that when Paul was calling them to establish a legal and godly soul tie. Having a kindred spirit is like identical twins who think alike. I can attest to that because I have a twin brother, and we think alike often.

We formulate soul ties through the involvement of our mind, will, and emotions. This is how they are created. It is a collaborating, marrying, and knitting of the souls. There are godly soul ties and ungodly ones. Marriage is a godly and ordained soul tie. We must understand that whenever we engage in sexual intercourse it establishes a soul tie. Any verbal or written agreement between two or more parties becomes a soul tie. We have to understand the importance of soul ties and how they work in our lives, whether godly or ungodly ones.

Becoming One Flesh: A Body Tie

There is also a "body tie" that is connected to the soul when someone makes up their mind to be intimate with another. Being intimate with someone outside of marriage will create a body-soul tie or "one flesh bonding." Sexual intercourse outside of marriage is sin called fornication in the eyes of God. The apostle Paul also dealt with this sternly in his letter to the Corinthian church:

Do you not know that he who unites himself with a prostitute is one with her in body? For it is said, "The two will become one flesh" (1 Corinthians 6:16 NIV).

In the above passage of Scripture we see that a soul tie is linked to a body tie. When you have sexual intercourse with someone—anyone outside of marriage, not just a prostitute—a soul tie and a body tie are established. Let me paint a picture for you of what an ungodly soul tie looks like. We have heard stories of women who are dating or married to men who are domineering, jealous, and controlling. He demands that she not have any friends, isolates her from her relatives, and takes away her phone and keys to keep her monitored. What goes on in people's minds? Why in the world is she still with him or married to that type of person? Why does she not seek outside help when he leaves?

Furthermore, we have heard many stories about abusive relationships where there is domestic violence between a man and a woman. We ponder why the woman does not leave the abusive boyfriend or husband. Oftentimes we hear these types of answers and excuses: "I love him; I can't leave him; I'm afraid to leave; he will kill me." I believe this illustrates my point and is a perfect example of an individual whose mind, will, emotions are taken advantage of by control, domination, manipulation, and physical, mental, and verbal abuse. Their soul has been taken over by another, which creates an ungodly soul tie. We can see by this example the negative impact to a person's mind, will, and emotions.

Anything that takes control of one's mind, will, and emotions may be an ungodly, illegal, and unhealthy soul tie. I must say that when soul ties, body ties, and spirit ties are established they are not just natural but also spiritual. When I think about soul ties, I think about a covenant relationship that is established between two or more people. There are many soul wars happening in people lives. People are bound by other people's decisions over their lives.

Never allow anyone to think for you. Take ownership over your own soul. Free yourself from any toxic relationships, connections, and alliances that produces spiritual barrenness and that are ungodly. God is a covenant God! We are bound by what we speak. We can also free ourselves with what we speak. That is why the tongue is a powerful instrument. We must establish covenant relationships in the kingdom that are kindred, like-hearted, like-minded, and identically souled.

The Bible says, *"Can two walk together, except they be agreed?"* (Amos 3:3). Soul ties are established by mutual agreement, whether written or verbal. They become what I call a "soul decree." What we speak and decide by our own will and emotions will establish a soul decree. This is why Christian believers must be led by the Spirit of God, have the mind of Christ, be sober-minded, have the wisdom of God, and have patience—so that their decision is not driven by their own desires or appetites or controlled by anyone else. We must pray that God establishes godly ties in our lives spiritually, socially, and in marriage. These are godly covenant relationships or friendships that God establishes.

Jonathan and David's Covenant Relationship

I am reminded of the controversy over David and Jonathan's relationship. Traditional religious interpretation of their friendship is that it was a platonic love, while mainstream media sometimes considers it an example of homosexuality. We know this view is far from the truth and contrary to the ways of God and total violation of God's Word. There are Universalist teachers who build their worldview, premise, and validation of their sexual orientation and lifestyle on this one particular story. They assume that David and Jonathan were involved in a romantic relationship.

There is no evidence or biblical support of such involvement. David and Johnathan had a godly soul tie. It was a covenant relationship. It was an intimate but platonic relationship or friendship between two men. It was a true love that they had with each other. Let us look clearly at what the Bible says about their relationship and not pervert it to fix or justify a lifestyle or sexual orientation:

> *As soon as he had finished speaking to Saul, the soul of Jonathan was knit to the soul of David, and Jonathan loved him as his own soul. And Saul took him that day and would not let him return to his father's house. Then Jonathan made a covenant with David, because he loved him as his own soul* (1 Samuel 18:1-3 ESV).

Obviously, there is nothing in the above context relating to homosexuality. We can see that there was a mutual knitting of the souls of these men as they encountered each other. This does not allude to love at first sight or that they were potential soul mates. It was more like an extended family. Jonathan and David, I believe, were seeing each other as brothers and close friends. Have you ever been accepted into a friend's family and they called you their brother or sister? Or have you met someone and felt like you had known them all your life? There was a kindred spirit and knitting of their heart. This was a legal and godly soul tie. It was a covenant relationship. Jonathan loved David as his own soul. David was received into Saul's home like a son.

In other words, Saul adopted David, and Jonathan loved him as himself. He protected David as he would protect himself. We can see that Jonathan made a covenant with David because He loved David as his own soul. A true soul tie that God establishes is based on *agape* love from the premise of a covenant. Christian believers are to love each other as God loves us and as we love ourselves. Oftentimes, there are true, genuine relationships that God establishes in our lives, but over time they can become perverted if not prayed through.

Most churches do not educate the saints about the power of soul ties, word curses, generational curses, demons, and the kingdom of darkness. There are doors and entryways that are opened out of ignorance and through sin. We have to learn how to renounce word curses, sever illegal and ungodly soul ties, and shut doors that have been opened.

Did you know that when a person has multiple sexual partners, a soul tie is established with each and every one, whether they were in love with them or not? In other words, if a person had sexual encounters with six individuals that person will have now established soul ties and body ties with all six people. A relationship that is not legal or ordained by marriage still establishes a soul tie with the individual for a lifetime, until a physical separation happens and the act of sin is renounced. Then the soul tie can be broken and reversed.

Residence of the Holy Spirit

The apostle Paul understood and taught the importance of keeping our vessels as sacred and pure before the Lord. Our bodies become the residence of the Holy Spirit. We are to protect our spiritual houses and bodies from anything that will desecrate them when they are to be consecrated. This is also why men and women who engage in homosexuality, adultery, and prostitution become bound, addicted, and entangled in their spirits to that lifestyle. We must make a conscious decision of what we do with our body and soul because even our bodies can become a gateway to the Holy Spirit or to evil tormenting spirits.

There are those who have been molested, raped, and violated unwillingly and need to have the soul tie and body tie broken by the Holy Spirit. Those who have been violated and go throughout life bitter, angry, fearful, confused, lost, and depressed never really get the breakthrough that they so desperately need. There is, however, healing and deliverance through the blood of Jesus Christ, who will restore innocence and virginity.

There are relational issues that take place because of unfaithfulness, infidelity, adultery, and fornication through seduction. Have you ever met someone who is unable to commit to one individual and has a hard time settling down with one person? Or have you heard about what are now called "open" relationships? One of the primary reasons is that a soul tie has been created by past relationships, lovers, and partners and has not been severed. Whether the relationship ended well or badly, the person struggles to move on and usually compares new relationships with the old relationship because they never got set free. Once the relationship has ended, it is so painful and often extremely difficult to establish a close-knit relationship with another person. Soul ties have memory, and breaking them will purge all that from the database of the spirit.

The three words "I love you!" are more powerful than we think, and those words have forcible power to influence a person's mind, will, and emotions. A person can be in love with a past lover while in a new relationship. Loving a past lover has been the cause of many breakups. A person must break the old soul attachment before they can create a new one. That does not always happen because people are not aware of the spiritual influence that soul ties and body ties can have. Just because a new relationship is created does not mean the old relationship is completely over. There is still a part that remains joined with the previous lover, causing emotions to become fragmented (see 1 Cor. 6:16).

Marriage Is a Godly Soul Tie and Body Tie

Has not the one God made you? You belong to him in body and spirit. And what does the one God seek? Godly offspring. So be on your guard, and do not be unfaithful to the wife of your youth (Malachi 2:15 NIV).

As we have learned, soul ties and body ties are spiritual and are meant to describe a covenant relationship bond that exists on earth between two people and is paralleled in the heavenly realms. We must understand the significance of a soul and body tie that is spiritual and for the purpose of joint covenant. The soul ties between two people are usually mutually beneficial, like a two-way street or like an umbilical cord between an infant and its mother, which has a two-way blood flow. God looks at a legal soul tie, body tie, and spirit tie as a means of mutual support, nurturing, love, and ordained covenant in His order.

There is also an eternal spirit tie, I call it, that was established when we gave our lives to Jesus. Jesus understood that His spiritual nourishment was to do the will of the Father who sent Him. His mission was to finish the Father's work. Jesus' purpose was to destroy the work of the devil by causing prophetic breakthrough to take place as He broke the power of the devil. As disciples of Christ, we are being nurtured by the Word of God and through the Holy Spirit who resides in us, who feeds us God's eternal purpose for our lives. It is the spiritual umbilical cord between Heaven and earth.

Unfortunately, the enemy will always pervert, twist, and confuse God's order into an ungodly order. Individuals can also establish between them ungodly soul ties in the spiritual realm. The enemy loves this because this creates an opportunity for him pervert, corrupt, control, manipulate, and weaken both individuals. In modern society, especially in America, pornography, sexting, and reality television shows that endorse sex are big business and produce revenue. Media has been a catalyst that supports "liberated sex," and the enemy uses this engine to seduce, deceive, and control hundreds of thousands and millions of people around the world.

Illicit soul ties are established every day, and there is a soul war going on as well as a spiritual war of the mind, will, and emotions. That is why we need to put on the whole armor of God in this hour. God's original intent was that soul ties, spirit ties, and body ties are designed as two-way channels of blessing, covenant, and nurturing in the life of the believer. A soul tie is like a three-stranded umbilical cord that is created in the spiritual realm. There are also ungodly yokes that we place upon ourselves that must be broken in order for us to receive our prophetic breakthrough. God's yoke is easy and His burden is light. We have to make sure that we carry the yoke and burden of the Lord and not things that will hinder us from walking in our divine purpose.

God wants to set us free from the strings of attachments that are in the invisible realm. I always say that prophetic words from God can bring prophetic breakthrough. I believe that one prophetic word from God can remove and break a lifetime of labor. Jesus came to destroy the works of the devil. Strongholds, word curses, generational curses, ungodly soul ties, poverty, confusion, deception, sickness, and disease are the works of satan that he uses to kill, steal, and destroy your destiny. We are not satan's puppet on a string.

Jesus Sets the Captive Free

We know that Jesus is the chain-breaker, and who the Son sets free is free indeed. Jesus will cut ties and ungodly cords that have been established unknowingly and knowingly. Jesus can and will cut these evil cords and bonds if we ask Him to, but we have obligations as well—to allow Jesus to assist us to a place of total freedom. Keep in mind that the depressed, oppressed, weak, vulnerable, spiritually broken, financially distressed, and the physically sick, disabled, lame, crippled, and emotionally drained are oftentimes bound by these things. The power of God can break every chain.

Confess Our Sin to Bring Healing

There is freedom from the strongholds of life when we are transparent and honest with ourselves. Confession is a powerful thing when done with a pure heart. If we confess our sins unto the Lord, He is faithful and just to forgive us from all of them and purify us. Healing is connected to receiving breakthrough through confession.

> *If we confess our sins, he is faithful and just and will forgive us our sins and purify us from all unrighteousness* (1 John 1:9 NIV).

Confess your trespasses to one another, and pray for one another, that you may be healed. The effective, fervent prayer of a righteous man avails much (James 5:16 NKJV).

Repentance Will Break Ungodly Patterns

Turning away from any ungodly sin and lifestyle will keep us free from any open doors. Repentance is key to a mature believer making the right decision and shunning evil.

I tell you, no! But unless you repent, you too will all perish (Luke 13:5 NIV).

Forgiveness Will Keep You Free

There is another lethal weapon that the enemy uses that becomes a stronghold and a hard-to-break soul tie—bitterness, resentment, offense, unforgiveness, and hatred. Unforgiveness is something the devil loves to use to keep a soul tie in place. We must learn how to forgive quickly and love those who may have trespassed and offended us. As Christian believers, we have to learn how to show mercy and exhibit love and compassion. People often have a hard time letting go of the past or people because of unforgiveness, which is a soul tie that must be destroyed.

There are open doors and unhealthy soul ties that will fall off and close automatically when we release, renounce, and detach ourselves from those who have wronged, offended, and hurt us. I have learned that saying "I'm sorry" can go a long way even if it's not your fault. I have seen tremendous breakthrough in my own life when I have forgiven people and prayed that God will bless them. Forgiveness is a powerful weapon against the enemy, and unforgiveness is a counter-weapon against the saints of God.

For if you forgive other people when they sin against you, your heavenly Father will also forgive you. But if you do not forgive others their sins, your Father will not forgive your sins (Matthew 6:14-15 NIV).

God knows exactly what happened, but we must arise and set an example to walk in love and forgiveness. It is hard to do at times, but ask the Lord for wisdom to teach you through His Word and with the help of Holy Spirit. Love will teach a believer how to forgive. It is imperative for our spiritual welfare and health to forgive those who have abused, offended, violated, wronged, or dominated us through fear and manipulation. Moreover, activating forgiveness to those who have taken advantage of us in ungodly relationships of any kind is an essential foundation for severing the bonds that illegally tie us to others.

I have been ministering in prophetic deliverance where it was difficult to set a person free because of a root of unforgiveness established in their heart. As I identify the areas of hurt, shame and guilt by walking the individual in to confessing, renouncing, and acknowledging where the bitterness rooted from, the person is totally set free. Ungodly soul ties of any kind are one of the most common strategies or methods that the devil uses to hold people in spiritual bondage or captivity. What I have shared in this chapter is just a basic guide that will assist you in understanding how to break ungodly soul ties.

Here are *five* simple steps that one can utilize to break ungodly soul ties so that they can be the recipient of perpetual breakthrough in their lives. Any dark areas of our soul must be confronted with the Word of God, and the light of His kingdom will shine through.

Five Steps to Breaking Ungodly Soul Ties

Step One: Repent

One of the first steps that must not be overlooked is repenting of any sinful act or involvement with any one person or persons. Be honest with yourself by confessing to the Lord—whether it was adultery, fornication, etc. It is vital that a person repent of those sins and embrace the Father's love and forgiveness for that act. This must be done first before a person can move on in breaking any soul tie. Acknowledging, repenting, and turning away from the act of sin is key in receiving breakthrough and walking in prophetic purpose in Christ.

Step Two: Forgive

One of the hardest things to do is forgive a person for what has happened. In addition, loving the unlovable is another thing to do, especially if one has been offended, hurt, abused, used, manipulated, etc. To break a soul tie, one must forgive the person or persons of any wrongdoing. If there is hidden unforgiveness of any kind in one's soul and heart against a person, they must decide to release that resentment, bitterness, unforgiveness, grudge, and issue and forgive them of any and all wrong that has occurred against them. We must understand that the Bible says that bitterness can defile a man.

Step Three: Renounce

There is power in the words that we speak. We know that death and life are in the power of the tongue. We must exercise our spiritual rights as king-priests by renouncing any and all covenants made with the person we established a soul tie with. Just as a soul tie is created through verbal and written agreement and other acts of mutual covenant, one can break it through the same means.

Words like "I will love you forever" or "You belong to me" are verbal commitments, vows, or covenants that become decrees in the spiritual realm that bind one soul to another, which automatically creates a soul tie. That is why we must be careful what we speak, especially from a hurt place in our heart. The tongue has the ability and capability to create soul ties by what we speak out of our mouths.

Thou art snared with the words of thy mouth, thou art taken with the words of thy mouth (Proverbs 6:2 KJV).

In order for ungodly soul ties to be broken, we must use the power of the tongue to renounce those spoken covenants, commitments, pledges, and vows. When a person renounces something, they are actually reversing what was previously spoken. In other words, when you speak something verbally, you have to power to take it back verbally by the power of God. For example, if a woman had a soul tie with a man and found out later that he was not the one for her, and due to the bad relationship she spoke out of her mouth that she would never love another man, then this needs to be renounced if she wants to break the soul tie in her life. Remember that we are snared by the words of our own mouth.

This same woman could renounce and reverse what she said by saying something along the line of "I renounce having said that I will never be able to love another man," and "I release myself remove any and all trauma, pain, resentment, hurt, bitterness, and judgment against him in Jesus' name." If there are things you cannot recall, that is okay; just renounce anything you can remember and ask God to break any words that snared you and that you established verbally out of ignorance or knowingly.

Step Four: Remove

I believe that a major stronghold that people in general struggle with is letting go of things given to them by past relationships. Material possessions often remind a person of a time, season, and moment in their lives. Gifts, monies, clothing, jewelry, pet animals, cars, houses, etc. become a link to a person whether they have moved on or not. What I am about to say may be hard to swallow, but one must get rid of any gifts exchanged. Now, having children with a person is not something you can exchange—that is a gift from the Lord. I am not talking about children but gifts that represent a past relationship that can reinforce that soul tie.

Gifts exchanged can often symbolize a relationship and can hold a soul tie in place regardless of whether the relationship has ended. We must understand the power of what a soul tie represents. We must throw away, remove, and discard anything that triggers old thoughts, emotions, and feelings. If you have rings, monetary gifts, personal gifts, cards, jewelry, and other relationship gifts from a previous relationship, then now is the time to clean house and remove them out of your possession.

We have to understand that holding on to such gifts symbolizes that the relationship is still in good standing and can actually hold the soul tie in place even after it has been renounced. After repenting, forgiving, and removing any material items, the last step is renouncing by announcing the ungodly and illegal soul tie specifically and then breaking it by the sword of the Spirit and the Word of God.

Step Five: Renounce by Announcing

The last step to severing the soul tie is verbally renouncing its existence in your life and then just breaking it in Jesus' name. I believe in prophetic acts as a prophetic leader. I would actually use my fingers as scissors, and as I renounce and pray I'd imagine that the soul tie is cut, severed, and broken. I also used to take martial arts, and I would karate chop while renouncing a soul tie. There is power in demonstration, and I would usually feel the Spirit of God come upon me when I act it out by faith. Every soul tie that God would recall to my memory I would cut off and break the cord in the spirit. It may seem very strange and dramatic to do, but it works.

Let me tell you a funny story. When my mother used to discipline me for being disobedient as a child, she would talk to me and spank me at the same time. It was not funny when my mother chastened me, but later I truly understood why she had to discipline me that way. Being a young boy living in a rough environment, it worked because of her love for me: "I am doing what God called me to do." That tough love at times broke bad habits that I had. She would verbally tell me why she spanked me. It hurt her to do it more than it hurt me, but it was needed. My point is that we have to verbally sever and even act it out at the same time by using a demonstration of cutting the cord, string, or tie. We must understand that verbally renouncing something carries a lot of weight in the spiritual realm. Likewise, when vows are exchanged that bind the soul, renouncing can release the soul from bonds.

Spiritual Prayer to Break Ungodly Soul Ties

The Bible clearly says that what we bind on earth is bound in Heaven and what we loose will be loosed in Heaven (the heavenly or spiritual realm). As Christian believers, you can renounce and loose yourself from all ungodly soul ties by simply speaking something like this from your heart:

I now renounce and loose myself from any and all ungodly soul ties formed, created, established, between myself and _____, and I break its power, influence, control, rule, and every ungodly soul tie in my life in Jesus' name.

> *Do not be unequally yoked with unbelievers. For what partnership has righteousness with lawlessness? Or what fellowship has light with darkness?* (2 Corinthians 6:14 ESV)

Part Two

90-DAY
DEVOTIONAL
and
Activations to
Release Blessings
and Break Curses

Day 1

Psalm 79:9

*Help us, O God of our salvation! Help us for
the glory of your name. Save us and forgive
our sins for the honor of your name.*

God's Name Is Always Glorified

As you launch into deep waters, keep this in mind—the deeper
the waters, the greater your faith will be challenged. You will rise
up and swim above adversity instead of being swept along with the
current and dragged down by the waves. I am aligning your mind,
body, and soul with My perfect will. My child, do you have any
idea what is in store for those who trust their God? I smile with
great appreciation as I watch you enter into a place of stability. You
are learning to make wise decisions regarding your destiny.

You have known people who have fallen short of their personal
goals and dreams due to an unexpected turn of events. Change is
inevitable. You can benefit from change if you refuse to settle for
less than My best. I am the God of your salvation, who saved you
to deliver others as Moses did. I have put My stamp of approval
upon you. If you have any questions, do not hesitate to ask Me.
You know where to find Me. I will move Heaven and earth to respond to your needs. You are not alone. I am by your side always.

Scriptures
Matthew 14:29; 2 Corinthians 1:22, 5:7;
Romans 12:2; Philippians 4:19

Breakthrough Prayer

I glorify You with my lips. Everything I do and all that I am reflects Your love, joy, and creativity. You fashioned me to worship You and reflect Your splendor and glory in the earth. I am living proof of Your powerful presence. I desire that Your blessings overflow to others. In Jesus' name, I pray. Amen.

BREAKING CURSES AND RELEASING BLESSINGS
Day 1

I decree and release the favor of God on my life and that Jesus is glorified in every area.

I destroy and break all spoken curses and negative words that I have spoken over my life and family.

I decree and release the light of the kingdom of God to shine in dark places that I may go.

I destroy and break all spoken curses and negative words that others have spoken over my life and family.

I decree and release uncommon favor and justice that will give me access to succeed.

I destroy and break every ungodly pattern, mindset, and resistance that is against my destiny.

I decree and release the strength to rebuild the wall and repair the breaches (see Isa. 58:12).

I destroy, annul, and break all ungodly covenants, oaths, pledges, contracts, and alliances that I have made verbally.

I decree and declare that my blessing is never held up by demonic systems, governments, and organizations in Jesus' name.

Day 2

Psalm 86:4-5

Give me happiness, O Lord, for I give myself to you. O Lord, you are so good, so ready to forgive, so full of unfailing love for all who ask for your help.

God Wants Revival to Begin with You

Awake, awake from your slumber! I am your daily alarm clock. Your spirit connects with Mine. I am ready when you are to move forward. My beloved, I am overjoyed that every day you have purposed to walk in your destiny. Don't stop until you've done everything you set your mind to achieve. You have a winning attitude that many people might not expect or understand. You are called to provide strength to some and advice, counsel, and wisdom to others. Regardless of your age, background, or experience, I have given you the intelligence and personality that attracts attention.

Avoid self-criticism. It only detains you from advancing and expanding your sphere of influence. Time to enlarge your territory, break free from the familiar, and venture into the great unknown. Remember Jabez? He prayed for Me to enlarge his territory, increase him on every side, and provide protection against wickedness. Just as Jabez did, ask for My all-encompassing blessing. You should make this your daily request, My child. Expect Me to do just that and more for you.

Scriptures
Psalm 121:4; 2 Corinthians 2:14; 1 Chronicles 4:10; Deuteronomy 2:7, 15:10, 28:12; Philippians 4:6-7

Breakthrough Prayer

My words matter. I want to make declarations and decrees according to Your promises. Father, make known the secrets that are part of my inheritance. Bless the works of my hands and allow me to continue producing good fruit. In Jesus' name. Amen.

BREAKING CURSES AND RELEASING BLESSINGS
Day 2

I decree and release personal revival of the Holy Spirit in my life.

I destroy and break all resistance to the move of the Spirit and to truth and any antichrist spirit.

I decree and release the oil of the Spirit that will impact, transform, and revolutionize those I meet.

I destroy and break any breaches in my life that would give satan and demons access, in Jesus' name.

I decree and release the power of the Spirit of God on my life that will position me to stand and make up the hedge (see Ezek. 22:30).

I destroy, renounce, and break all crooked speech that would cause a breach (see Prov. 15).

I decree and release revival that will be my portion, and every dry place will be soaked, drenched, and saturated with God's presence.

I destroy and break every curse and hoax against the work of the Holy Spirit in my life.

I decree that I am fully armored with the armor of God in Jesus' name (see Eph. 6:11).

Day 3

Psalm 86:15

*But you, O Lord, are a God of compassion
and mercy, slow to get angry and filled
with unfailing love and faithfulness.*

God Is Full of Compassion

When you sleep, your mind is racing. I am aware of what's on your heart. I watch you as you toss and turn at night, unable to fall back asleep. I have seen you press through life's pressure and remain unbreakable. No one knows what is deep inside you. If you shared about your trials and troubles, no one would believe you, so you stay silent. You keep your pain and struggles to yourself. My child, I will intervene for you supernaturally.

What concerns you concerns Me. Many times, you have remarked that you do not have enough, and when you do have enough something else happens that needs your undivided attention. You have also said it is always one thing after another that stresses you out. I am breaking that cycle. It's up to you to go to the next level. My love for you leaves no room for shame, condemnation, or operating under your own muscle and might. You give generously and often get nothing in return. I am the Giver of every good and perfect gift. Believe I am placing provisions in your hands today.

Scriptures

Acts 17:11; 1 Thessalonians 5:18;
Hebrews 9:19; Ephesians 1:4-5

Breakthrough Prayer

How grateful I am for Your goodness and Your grace. You empower me with wisdom, revelation knowledge, and discernment. I am in awe of Your all-consuming love and compassion for me. Your restoration and healing power recovers what's been missing in my life and releases miracles. I know that each day that I am Your idea! In Jesus' name. Amen.

BREAKING CURSES AND RELEASING BLESSINGS
Day 3

I decree and release the love of Christ in my life that will bring about change.

I destroy and break ungodly agendas, motives, objectives, and persuasions that come to distract, alter, and sabotage the purpose of God in my life.

I decree and release the compassion of Christ that will bring deliberate breakthroughs in those I encounter daily.

I destroy and break every spirit sent to destroy and silence my voice.

I decree and release angelic protection and surveillance around my property, possessions, family, finances, friends, ministry, church, city, and community.

I destroy and break every chain of resistance and illegal soul ties established verbally and contractually.

I destroy, renounce, and break all false idols, deities, and vain worship in Jesus' name.

I decree and declare that the Lord of the breaker will turn every word curse spoken against my life into sevenfold blessings in Jesus' name.

I destroy and break every false or pretentious love, affection, passion, and desire.

I decree and release upon my life full restitution with interest and restoration to come suddenly in Jesus' name.

Day 4

Psalm 86:17

*Send me a sign of your favor. Then those
who hate me will be put to shame, for
you, O Lord, help and comfort me.*

God Sends Signs When Asked

Be ready in season and out of season, My dear one. There will be times when you will be called into action, whether it is convenient or inconvenient. I will say to you, My child—about face! Are you ready to fight back? I am with you, soldier, and I have gone before you as the Commanding Officer. Preparation is critical to fulfill what is required. Like the military, a good soldier must be ready to report for duty. That is why you are enrolled in boot camp. I am training, equipping, and preparing you for service. You never know what opportunities and possibilities will open up for you. I don't want you to miss out on what you have been praying and waiting for.

Prepare yourself to step into your passion, call, dream, and work. I will give you favor with people. I will make your opposition witness the power of your God and Father. Watch as I touch hearts and change mindsets in your favor. I know the outcome of everything that occurs. I will embarrass those who hate My kingdom and highly esteem those who know and love Me. Many will see My hand working in your day-to-day life. Like a billboard, your success announces My favor over your life.

Scriptures

2 Timothy 4:2; Ezekiel 36:26; 1 Peter 5:6; James 4:10

Breakthrough Prayer

You are the Master Teacher. Thank You, Jesus, for revealing Your ways and pointing me to the best path to follow. Strengthen my spirit. Father, I want to obey and adhere to Your good and perfect will. Show me how to navigate pitfalls and potholes strategically placed by the enemy to stall my spiritual growth. I am determined to execute Your will. In Jesus' name. Amen.

BREAKING CURSES AND RELEASING BLESSINGS
Day 4

I decree and release signs, wonders, and miracles that accompany me in my daily activities.

I destroy and break false signs, wonders, and miracles that come to deceive.

I decree and release that my gates are praise and walls be salvation (see Isa. 60:18).

I destroy, bind, and break up all my breaches in Jesus' name (see Isa. 30:26).

I decree and release angelic assistance that will bring me into my wealthy place.

I destroy and break every power of darkness that comes to rob me, my family, my loved ones, and the relationship of what is rightfully mine.

I decree and release the heavens to open up over my life and pour down blessings from above.

I destroy, renounce, and break false gifts, ministry, prophets, and organizations that are sent from hell, in Jesus' name.

I decree and release the supernatural work of God that is demonstrated through my life to bring perpetual impact.

Day 5

Psalm 91:1-2

Those who live in the shelter of the Most High will find rest in the shadow of the Almighty. This I declare about the Lord: He alone is my refuge, my place of safety; he is my God, and I trust him.

God's Shadow Offers Shelter

Live in My presence. Hide yourself in My shadow. For it is in My presence that you are protected from the enemy attacks. The enemy despises you for surrendering your life and will to Me. Resting in My shadow, you will gain your strength, power, and authority. I am your Light. When do shadows appear? They are only produced when there is light. I am your Defender. Nothing and no one can get past My watchful eyes. Know that I have you where I want you. Sit back, relax, and find solace in My shadow. Never fear the shadow of death because in Christ, My child, you will see that it is only a shadow after all. There is no need to fear. The enemy is already a defeated foe. The enemy is your foe and I am your Friend.

In Egypt, the death angel—known as the destroyer—passed over the doors and homes of those who painted their doorposts with blood. Understand today that I am your Passover. Nothing in your life will destroy you because Jesus' blood and sacrifice covered your sins and protected you from death, harm, and devastation. Trust Me this morning to protect you from the unforeseen dangers that come to persecute those who belong to Me. Remain confident that I am your Safe Haven.

Scriptures

John 8:12; 1 Corinthians 5:7; Exodus 12:23; 1 Peter 1:18-19; 1 John 1:7

Breakthrough Prayer

You are my Shelter and my Refuge, protecting me from rain, storms, winter blizzards, and hurricanes of life. You are my Defender! I am certain that You will safeguard my soul. When I am afraid, I expect my faith will override my fears and flood my soul with Your abiding peace. I pray in Jesus' name. Amen.

BREAKING CURSES AND RELEASING BLESSINGS
Day 5

I decree and release the shadow of God that will bring about miracles and healings to others.

I destroy and break the powers of the shadows of death, the grave, and hell in Jesus' name.

I decree and release the unprecedented grace and anointing to destroy all ungodly yokes and burdens.

I destroy and break the powers of witches, warlocks, false prophets, physics, charismatic witchcraft prayers, thoughts, ideas, projections, warfare, portals, all natural artifacts, powers, sorcery, magic, voodoo, all manipulation, and mind control in Jesus' name.

I decree and release breakthrough prayers that will advance me in the things of the Spirit.

I destroy and break every power of demonic and satanic jinxes, potions, incantations, chanting, crystals, root works, eggs, scorpions, serpents, spiders, creatures, and false prophecies sent against me, my family, my body, my church, my friends, my possessions, and my mind in Jesus' name.

Day 6

Psalm 91:3-4

For he will rescue you from every trap and protect you from deadly disease. He will cover you with his feathers. He will shelter you with his wings. His faithful promises are your armor and protection.

God's Protection from Deadly Things

The enemy hates your guts and the very fact that you are still alive and living on the earth. He hated the fact that My Son, Jesus, was born. His existence troubled all of hell because it signaled the long-awaited King and Rule had arrived. On the day that Heaven announced your birth, the enemy began to plot against *you*. Do not worry or be afraid. I have not given you a spirit of fear and timidity but of power, love, and self-control. Know that I have given you the power to tread on serpents, scorpions, and any of the enemy's deadly messengers.

For in this season, My child, it's time that you stomp your foot down on the enemy of your destiny. Schemes and traps have been set up against you, but I will tear them down. I will hide you in the feathers of My wings—a mighty shield covering you from head to toe. Never will I renege on My Word or rescind My precious promises for your life. As the battle wages on, My covering will serve as an impenetrable armor, protecting you against the blows of the enemy.

Scriptures

Revelation 1:6, 5:10; 1 Peter 2:9; 2 Timothy 1:7;
Psalm 31:4, 57:6, 91:4, 141:9

Breakthrough Prayer

Father, each and every day let me clearly see that the tongue wields the power of life and death. I know there are deadly plots and word curses designed for me. I will steer clear of ungodly influences and corrupt communication. You are my strong armor and my protector. Shelter me safely underneath Your wings. In Jesus' name. Amen.

BREAKING CURSES AND RELEASING BLESSINGS
Day 6

I decree and release the life of Christ flowing through my veins in the spirit.

I destroy and break any demonic attacks that will bring premature death and accidents in Jesus' name.

I decree and release the healing rivers and fountain of youth provided by God's Word.

I destroy, expose, and break all ill wishes, word curses, demonic plots, plans, tactics, and strategies of the enemy in Jesus' name.

I decree and release the strength of an ox and ant, keen vision and agility of an eagle, boldness and power of a lion.

I destroy and break every dark art, spirit of perversion, and confusion that tries to deceive and blind my perception in Jesus' name.

I decree and release the power to make wise decisions that will set the pace of my destiny.

I destroy and break ungodly habits, thirst, and hunger in Jesus' name.

Day 7

Psalm 91:5-7

Do not be afraid of the terrors of the night, nor the arrow that flies in the day. Do not dread the disease that stalks in darkness, nor the disaster that strikes at midday. Though a thousand fall at your side, though ten thousand are dying around you, these evils will not touch you.

God Safeguards You from Harm

Good morning, My mighty one. I want you to understand that there are new places, people, and things that you will soon encounter. You wanted a fresh and brand-new way of approaching things. Now, there is nothing wrong with that. I desire for you to come into a new season. I like new things and will give you "the new" and not something "recycled."

The enemy will barrage you with fiery darts when you least expect them. He engages in terrorist tactics to disrupt your life. The genocide that the devil threatens will not destroy your life. I will shelter you when the adversary's bombs are exploding. The battle belongs to Me. Be assured that no evil plot will stand. Nothing can withstand My armed forces.

Scriptures
1 Timothy 2:4; 2 Peter 3:9; Matthew 9:17;
Mark 2:22; Psalm 91:7-16

Breakthrough Prayer

No matter what situations I may face, no matter what trials and tribulations I encounter, I am committed to You, Almighty God. In You, I worship and pay homage. Worthy is the Lamb of God who has taken away my sins. I do not have to walk in fear or paranoia. In Your presence, You guarantee me protection and liberty. In Jesus' name, I pray. Amen.

BREAKING CURSES AND RELEASING BLESSINGS
Day 7

I decree and release the angelic host to surround me and protect me from evil.

I destroy, bind, and break any words of destruction against my calling and life in Jesus' name.

I decree and release the blessings that will bless others and position them to press past life circumstances.

I destroy, return, and break every demonic word curse sent and decree hundredfold blessings over that which was sent against me, my family, and life in Jesus' name.

I decree and release myself from any burdens or responsibilities placed upon myself out of ignorance or compromise.

I destroy, cut, burn, and break any ungodly silver cord, rope, soul tie, and lay line established illegally, in Jesus' name.

I decree and release covenant relationships and soul ties like David and Johnathan had in Jesus' name.

Day 8

Psalm 91:11-13

For he will order his angels to protect you wherever you go. They will hold you up with their hands so you won't even hurt your foot on a stone. You will trample upon lions and cobras; you will crush fierce lions and serpents under your feet!

God Orders His Angels to Fight for You

I want you to know, My beloved, whenever you need angelic assistance you can rely upon Me to dispatch them. My Son, Jesus, was betrayed by Judas and turned over to the authorities. Jesus could have prayed for an angel army to fight for Him. When you feel that you have been running into roadblocks, they do not define you or destroy your calling. Work with Me and not against your destiny.

You can fulfill your dreams when you hold on to My promises and My Word. When you feel overwhelmed or things start spinning out of your control, simply lift up your hands before Me. Let Me carry you to a place of rest. You must undergo a transition. Like an eagle, I will carry you on My wings, safeguarding you against roaring lions and venomous snakes that want to intimidate you. I will crush the fierce lions and cunning serpents under your feet.

Scriptures
PSALM 91:11; LUKE 4:10; EXODUS 23:20;
ACTS 26:14; GENESIS 3:15

Breakthrough Prayer

Father, as I come before You, establish the fear of the Lord in my heart. I will not compromise or get entangled with the spirit of the world. I know that I am a friend of God. Teach me to hear Your voice so that I may never fall for evil schemes. In Jesus' name. Amen.

BREAKING CURSES AND RELEASING BLESSINGS
Day 8

I decree that there is more with me than against me.

I destroy and break any accidents that will cause pain, agony, stress, and deaths in Jesus' name.

I decree and release the sound of abundance that will saturate my borders and territory.

I destroy and break any forces from hell that come to blackmail, resist, and bring false stigma against my name and integrity, in Jesus' name.

I decree and release the dew of Heaven to bring me that which is owed to me.

I destroy and break all sun and moon gods, deities, demons, and spirits operating through the sun, moon, or stars, in Jesus' name.

I decree and release hidden riches in secrets places to be used for kingdom advancements.

I destroy, bind, and break bands of darkness to keep me from prospering in season and out of season, in Jesus' name.

Day 9

Psalm 92:12

But the godly will flourish like palm trees and grow strong like the cedars of Lebanon.

God Will Strengthen You in Every Way

Good morning, My child. Make wise investments in your destiny. The seeds you plant today will grow into an abundant harvest tomorrow. I will make My children flourish like palm trees and become as sturdy and resolute as cedars. You will not fall by the wayside because I am strengthening and deepening your roots. As your roots spread out, they will determine the longevity and expansion of your tree trunk, which will be your foundation in Me.

If the enemy attempts to chop you down, I have equipped you with regenerating power. Learn from other trees how to maintain vitality and have long-lasting roots planted. This day, My child, I want to sharpen your edge so that you will remain relevant in these changing times. You will not become outdated but readily recognize My next move in the earth. Know that My Spirit will empower you to shed unwanted burdens.

Scriptures
GALATIANS 6:8; MATTHEW 3:10; LUKE 3:9;
2 KINGS 6:1-7; HEBREWS 8:13; LUKE 4:18; ISAIAH 61:1

Breakthrough Prayer

Father, let me demonstrate Your heart of love in everything that I do. I long to walk in cadence with You—not running ahead or lagging behind You. My desire is to be in the right place at the right time and with the right people doing the right thing and with the right agenda. Come, Holy Spirit, and help me recognize my Father's timing, so that I can remain in His will. When I am planted in the right soil, the Father will grow me up and prosper me. In Jesus' name. Amen.

BREAKING CURSES AND RELEASING BLESSINGS
Day 9

I decree that the breaker's anointing will be resident in my life.

I destroy, burn, and break every demonic womb, incubator, and conception created illegally in my life and those I relate to, in Jesus' name.

I decree and release promotion, bonuses, found money, unlimited favor, pardons, refunds, dividends, interest, exceptions, and recognitions.

I declare that the sun shall not smite me by day or the moon by night, in Jesus' name (see Ps. 121:6).

I decree and release the treasures of God within me to bless my generation.

I destroy, bind, disannul, and break all deities and demon spirits functioning through the stars and planets or astrological kingdom, in Jesus' name (see 2 Kings 23:5).

I decree and release hidden riches in secret places to be used for kingdom advancements.

Day 10

Psalm 92:14

Even in old age they will still produce
fruit; they will remain vital and green.

God Blesses You with Advanced Age

As you grow older and become more experienced, you will continue to be productive and fruitful. I will not allow you to become boring, uninterested, or passive. Moses' eyes never waned or dimmed. Know that I will cause your vision and dream to remain active and approachable. As seasons change, you will be able to accommodate what is needed to succeed. I am destroying the spirit of sabotage that attempts to steal the seeds you have sown. The fowls of the air search for seeds of greatness and swoop down to devour them. This will not happen to your seeds, My child.

Continue to be a good steward of the seeds you possess. I have placed within you seeds of greatness that are worth stewarding and preserving because they have the power to summon more than meets the eye. I will continue giving you assignments even as you age. Not only will you produce fruit from these but also those sowed in your youth. Your seeds will bring fruitfulness and blessings that will benefit others for years to come.

Scriptures
Deuteronomy 34:7; Ephesians 6:10-18;
Psalm 1:3, 92:14; Genesis 12:2

Breakthrough Prayer

May I not grow weary in doing good. I want to reap in due season and not faint. Father, deposit a greater revelation of Your life-giving promises. As I age, allow me to be sharper than ever before and prosper me beyond measure. Let me reap bountiful harvests in my advanced years as I did in the days of my youth. In Jesus' name. Amen.

BREAKING CURSES AND RELEASING BLESSINGS
Day 10

I decree that God will satisfy me with long life and great health.

I destroy and break premature occurrences that come to stop forward progression in life, ministry, business, and in every area.

I decree and release the ability to make spiritual decisions that will not forfeit the blessings of the Lord over my life.

I decree and declare that I am seated in heavenly places with Christ Jesus far above all principalities, power, might, dominion, and every name that is named (see Eph. 1:3).

I decree and release the gifts of the Holy Spirit within me to unlock the gifts and treasure pieces in others.

I destroy and break every brass heaven and iron gate over my life, in Jesus' name.

I decree and release an open heaven and bind up any satanic interference and interruption in Jesus' name.

Day 11

Psalm 94:18-19

*I cried out, "I am slipping!" but your
unfailing love, O Lord, supported me.
When doubts filled my mind, your comfort
gave me renewed hope and cheer.*

God's Unfailing Love Supports You

I know there are times when you feel unproductive. You may not see the progress that you desire, but be encouraged, My friend. Few dreams, visions, and callings happen overnight. The right season, timing, and connections can accelerate a new level of blessing. What you retain from Us in this season will signal the breakthrough you need to prepare yourself for trials and troubles.

We are here to help you get past your past. After all, the past is a classroom where valuable life lessons are taught. It can shape tomorrow's leaders and help them graduate into their callings. You are a born leader and an influential voice for this generation. We have come to dispel every doubt that clouds your mind and make it possible for you to realize your God-driven dreams. Cheer up, My special one, and know that everyone encounters trying times. Stealthily stealing your most holy faith is the enemy's game plan. Fix your eyes on Me and not the fear of the unknown. I am imparting renewed hope and unspeakable joy into your heart.

Scriptures
PSALM 19:3-4, 23:4; EPHESIANS 4:27;
JOHN 3:16; PROVERBS 13:12

Breakthrough Prayer

I have come to realize, Father, that You love those who love You. As I diligently pursue You, I discover Your unconditional love over and over again. You have supported me on my journey and never doubted that I would come into agreement with Your will. Yes, I am perplexed and indecisive at times, but You faithfully provide clarity when I need it. When I slip or fall away from You, it's Your voice that calls me back. In Jesus' name. Amen.

BREAKING CURSES AND RELEASING BLESSINGS

Day 11

I decree and release the love of God that will compel men unto to Jesus Christ.

I destroy and break the spirit of hatred that comes within my borders, in Jesus' name.

I decree and release the unconditional love of Christ that will win souls.

I destroy and break the spirit of sabotage, retaliation, revenge, vindication, and rage in Jesus' name.

I decree and release the heavens to bless my life.

I destroy and break the spirit of murder and assassination of my destiny and purpose.

I decree and pray for the angels of the Lord to be released to war against any spirit in the heavens assigned to block my prayers from being answered (see Dan. 10:12-13).

I destroy and break the spirit of divination—the python spirit that comes to hinder forward progress in Jesus' name.

Day 12

Psalm 94:22

But the Lord is my fortress; my God
is the mighty rock where I hide.

God Is Your Hiding Place

I sheltered Moses in the cleft of the rock and then passed by. That is where I revealed Myself. As Moses turned aside, I choose to speak with him in a burning bush, which is where I commissioned him and assigned him to deliver the Israelites. My child, you must turn aside if you wish to hear what I have planned next for your life's journey. Jeremiah did not think he was right for his assignment. Moses and Jeremiah did not think they was right for their assignments. They felt personal flaws and inadequacies disqualified them.

What you consider a personal flaw can turn into the very thing used for My glory. Do not doubt yourself or wish you were different. You are the person I desire to use to touch your generation. Why are you here? You are in the earth to fulfill what I have called you to do—influencing generation after generation as Moses and Jeremiah did. I desire for you to bring reformation and transformation to this fallen world.

Scriptures
EXODUS 33:22, 4:11; JEREMIAH 51:20; LUKE 15:20

Breakthrough Prayer

I thank You, Father, for choosing me in my mother's womb and calling me to be uniquely used in Your Kingdom. There have been times when I was not convinced of my calling, but You've replaced my insecurities with increasing faith and power. Whenever I feel vulnerable, You blanket me in Your warm and comforting presence. I know that I am accepted in the beloved. In Jesus' name, I pray. Amen.

BREAKING CURSES AND RELEASING BLESSINGS

Day 12

I decree and declare that my times are redeemed in the presence of God.

I destroy and break the enemy of my time in Jesus' name.

I decree and release the power of the anger of the Lord against the powers of darkness (see Ps. 90:11).

I destroy and break every stronghold of the adversary that keeps me from spending time in God's presence, in Jesus' name.

I decree and release the power and authority of the Lord now, against all demon spirits I encounter.

I destroy and break the spirit of allusions, false visons, demonic dreams, and false intuitions in Jesus' name.

I decree and release the power of the might of the Lord and Your hand that rules over my enemies (see 1 Chron. 29:12; Ps. 66:7).

I destroy and break the spirit of imitation and deception.

I destroy and release myself from the power of satan unto God through the blood of the Lamb, Jesus Christ (see Acts 26:18).

Day 13

Psalm 95:7

For he is our God. We are the people he watches over, the flock under his care. If only you would listen to his voice today!

God Attentively Listens to You

Do not get too comfortable where you are. There are stationary places in our lives. There are also times when we drift into complacency and lose our focus. We are what we think. Remember, My child, we can become consumed by the very culture that we want to escape from. When you are in trouble and find your back against the wall, know that I will make a way of escape. I am not your alternative nor am I plan B, but I am your *only* Way and Plan. Do not get stuck in the mud of chaos or rut of confusion. I will pull you out to bring you into something greater.

Know that I have pre-ordered your steps long before you were ever conceived in your mother's womb. Just as you pre-order new music, movies, books, and equipment, I have predetermined the pathway that will draw you closer to your destiny. I plan and care for who and what I have pre-ordered. Allow Me to expedite things on your behalf so you can arrive at the pre-ordained place of promise and destiny. You will discover once again that your Father has out done Myself. Along the way, you may encounter occasional hiccups and problems, but you will soon realize that I seal and deliver what I have pre-ordained.

Scriptures
James 1:22; John 15:1-27;
Ephesians 2:10; Genesis 15:5

Breakthrough Prayer

Holy Spirit, help me to stop questioning myself because this distracts me from my Father's direction and leading. Fine tune my ears to hear what the Spirit of the Lord is saying. Don't let my hearing become dull. Quiet my inner storms. Let me soak in my Father's presence. In Jesus' name, I pray. Amen.

BREAKING CURSES AND RELEASING BLESSINGS
Day 13

I decree and declare that my spriritual ears, eyes, and senses are open to the various ways that God speaks.

I destroy, silence, and break the deceptive voice of the enemy in Jesus' name.

I decree and release myself from any pressure placed on me by man.

I destroy and break every pillar of doubt, unbelief, and fear of the unknown and supernatural in Jesus' name.

I decree and release residual income and financial streams of wealth to build my vision.

I destroy and break the spirit of allusions, false visons, demonic dreams, and false intuitions in Jesus' name.

I decree and declare that I am strong in the power of God's might (see Eph. 6:10).

I destroy and break any false prophetic move, voice, or work of the enemy in Jesus' name.

I decree and release the power of the Holy Spirit to allow me to demonstrate daily what I have learned.

I destroy and break any words that come in my ears that will bring doubt of who I am in God.

Day 14

Psalm 97:10

*You who love the Lord, hate evil! He protects
the lives of his godly people and rescues
them from the power of the wicked.*

God Hates Evil and Protects You from Harm

I hand-picked you to be a leader of leaders. You were minding your business when suddenly I interrupted your plans. You may wonder why your desires and passions have suddenly changed. It is by My design. You have been perplexed, confused, and even upset at times that you could not do what you want when you want to do them. Know that I altered your plans and career goals, not the enemy. I do not want you to follow a path that you were never meant to pursue.

I did not want your talent or gifting to become your calling; instead, I wanted you to think of your calling as a mandate from Heaven to radically change the world. You are a world-changer and planet-shaker! The enemy is afraid of those who know their God and believe they will do great exploits. Godly exploits will become mighty explosions that will demolish the enemy's camp. My dear Son, Jesus, turned the culture upside down. Out with the old; time for the new.

Scriptures
Daniel 11:32; Romans 11:29;
Acts 2:4; Isaiah 43:19

Breakthrough Prayer

Purify my soul and imagination. Purify my heart and thoughts. Purify any motives that are not in agreement with Your will, Father. I want to be in right standing with You and become the righteousness of Christ. I know how much evil disgusts You. Deliver me from evil and the wicked one. In Jesus' name. Amen.

BREAKING CURSES AND RELEASING BLESSINGS
Day 14

I release myself from all evil and the roaming lion that comes to devour.

I break myself free from any plots and plans that are deadly and lethal, in Jesus' name.

I decree and release upon my life, family, friends, colleagues, relatives, spouse, and business partners the protection of the Lord.

I destroy and break any undercover and hidden agendas that are not God's plan and purpose, in Jesus' name.

I decree and declare that I will find safety under the shadow of God's wings.

I destroy and break the mischief, thief, and robbery spirit in Jesus' name.

I decree and release the power of Elijah through God's holy prophets.

I destroy and break the spirit of control, manipulation, trespassing, violation, and greed in Jesus' name.

Day 15

Psalm 97:11

*Light shines on the godly, and joy on
those whose hearts are right.*

God Knows Your Heart

Do not be afraid of the dark. After all, you are called into My marvelous light. I have saved you and delivered you from the enemy's snares. You have dominion, which means ruling, reigning, and reviving. Know this morning, My child, that My light shines on the righteous as well as those separated from Me and living in darkness. Let Me bring joy to your heart in the midst of pain and peace to your mind in the midst of confusion. I will overshadow you with My love in the midst of rejection, heartbreak, and hatred. I am shining Heaven's spotlight on you so others can see My goodness and favor on you.

Promotion and blessing are your inheritance. Learn from the prodigal son. He acquired all of his rights and inheritance as a son only to squander them. I will give you wisdom and what is rightfully yours in due season. I know how much you can handle. The prodigal son was not a prodigal. He lived his life like a fugitive not a beloved child. I am raising you up from the ashes and setting you on a solid foundation. The prodigal son lived in a pigpen as a result of his self-centered decisions. My child, you are not called to live like a pig. You are not a pig but you are My beloved, prized possession. I am restoring you to a place of prominence and honor.

Scriptures
Isaiah 41:10; Psalm 113:7; 1 Samuel 2:8; Luke 15:11-32;
1 Corinthians 6:10; Galatians 5:21

Breakthrough Prayer

Father, You know my heart better than anyone does. There is nothing hidden from You. Saturate me in Your amazing love. Point out anything that distracts me from doing what is acceptable in Your sight. My desire is to become Your love slave, Your worshiper. I am committed to You and only You. In Jesus' name, I pray. Amen.

BREAKING CURSES AND RELEASING BLESSINGS
Day 15

I release myself from any past hurt, resentment, unforgiveness, pain, memory, and obligation.

I destroy and break free from any obligation and agreement that wasn't the will of God.

I decree Your arm brings me into my inherited possession and You favor me (see Ps. 44:3).

I destroy and break every demonic influence that is purposed to slow me down, in Jesus' name.

I decree and declare that the angels of the Lord have charge over my life to deliver me (see Gen. 28:12; Ps. 91:11).

I destroy and break everything that is contrary to God's Word and voice in my life, in Jesus' name.

I decree and ask the Lord to release His angels to chase and persecute my enemies (see Ps. 35:5-6).

I destroy and break every crow, raven, vulture, or black bird of prey that comes to steal my possession—the prophetic word over my life and harvest—in Jesus' name.

I decree and release the angels the Lord to go before me and correct every crooked place.

I destroy and break myself free from any chains, fetters, cuffs, and ropes that restrict movement and liberty.

Day 16

Psalm 100:1-3

Shout with joy to the Lord, all the earth!
Worship the Lord with gladness. Come before
him, singing with joy. Acknowledge that the
Lord is God! He made us, and we are his.
We are his people, the sheep of his pasture.

God Loves Your Worship

I love when you worship Me and acknowledge My presence. I love to hear you sing your worship medley in your heart. I love when you worship, weep, and wail before Me. I know it is genuine and authentic. My child, you are My lodestar, the brightness in My universe. My overall plan has been to position spiritual representatives and offspring throughout the earth. I long to abide with My family and receive honor, esteem, and love from them.

Know that you are not alone even though your family and co-workers may at times misunderstand you. You are Mine. I created you. I know very well what upsets you. You are very special and dear to My heart. I personally want you to know that I love you. We have come to restore love that you have not felt in a very long time. I do understand when there are people around you and you still feel alone. Know that I am here for you. When you worship Me, I will turn your stress into rest. I am releasing you from anything that will hinder you from being who I have created you to be. You are My champion!

Scriptures
ACTS 17:29; JOHN 4:23-24; DEUTERONOMY 31:8;
1 JOHN 4:4; EPHESIANS 5:1

Breakthrough Prayer

Sharpen my spiritual senses each day, Father. I want to be aware of what's happening in the heavenlies. Let me experience Your presence in greater measure. Worship is not simply singing songs but a lifestyle for me. Give me a new song to sing to You. Help me to be a living sacrifice—holy and acceptable before You. In Jesus' name, I pray. Amen.

BREAKING CURSES AND RELEASING BLESSINGS
Day 16

I release myself from any hindrances, restraints, restrictions, and boundaries that prohibit free worship.

I destroy and break myself free from any music that is demonic, in Jesus' name.

I decree and ask God to answer by fire in every area that needs a spark.

I destroy and break any ungodly passions and feelings that are contrary to the Spirit of God, in Jesus' name.

I decree and declare that I am baptized with the Holy Spirit and fire (see Luke 3:16).

I destroy, drench, and extinguish false fire of the enemy in Jesus' name.

I decree and release the tongues of fire and angels.

I destroy and break any demonic language and tongues in Jesus' name.

I decree and release the fire of God that covers me around about (see Exod. 14:24).

I destroy and break any smoke screens and demonic firewalls.

Day 17

Psalm 102:17-18

He will listen to the prayers of the destitute.
He will not reject their pleas. Let this be
recorded for future generations, so that a
people not yet born will praise the Lord.

God Hears and Answers Your Prayers

Don't get frustrated, My child. I have not forgotten or turned a deaf ear to your petitions. I hear your prayers and I'm weighing your requests out. I know what you need long before you tell me. Now, I will not keep you waiting forever for your answer. I am always speaking and revealing Myself to you. Have you ever misplaced your keys, eyeglasses, or paperwork? After searching everywhere, you finally find the lost item sitting in front of you. The same holds true for the supernatural. You have been looking everywhere for answers only to find them inside your heart.

Do everything in total dependence on Me. Apart from Me, you can do nothing. Watch what we can do together. Trust that I will give you great advice that will bring the provision you need. It's terrible for your mind to be idle. Everything is not always a prayer away but just a thought away. Know that I am a just Judge who listens, cares, has compassion for the prayer requests of the destitute, and will not reject anyone's petition. Generations to come will witness My power and glory as I vindicate and restore those I love.

Scriptures
PHILIPPIANS 4:6; DEUTERONOMY 4:29; JEREMIAH 29:13;
2 THESSALONIANS 3:6; 1 PETER 4:13; ROMANS 8:17

Breakthrough Prayer

When I'm frustrated with myself and others, teach me to bring my emotions and concerns to You in prayer. I know You hear my daily petitions from Heaven and answer my prayers according to Your timetable not mine. I'm delighted that You don't look down on me. Forgive me, Father, when I spend more time complaining and grumbling than praying and declaring Your Word. May Your grace abound in my life. In Jesus' name, I pray. Amen.

BREAKING CURSES AND RELEASING BLESSINGS
Day 17

I decree and release the answers of the Lord to do what I was destined and called to do.

I destroy and break myself free from any voice that is contradictory to God's purpose, in Jesus' name.

I decree and release upon my life the keys of the kingdom that will open doors of favor.

I destroy and break myself free from any spirit that is sent to break godly covenants, in Jesus' name.

I decree and release arrows of the Lord to hit their bull's eye in my life.

I destroy and break the arrows of death sent and shot from the enemy camp.

I decree and release the arrows of the light of Your kingdom into the kingdom of darkness (see Hab. 3:11).

I destroy and break every ungodly rhythm in my life that comes to hinder growth and productivity, in Jesus' name.

I decree and release in my life the arrow of the Lord's deliverance to set me free (see 2 Kings 13:17).

I destroy and break in pieces the bows and arrows of death to my destiny.

Day 18

Psalm 103:1-4

Let all that I am praise the Lord; with my whole heart, I will praise his holy name. Let all that I am praise the Lord; may I never forget the good things he does for me. He forgives all my sins and heals all my diseases. He redeems me from death and crowns me with love and tender mercies.

God Forgives Sins and Heal Diseases

My child, today is your breakthrough! Why? Because you have awoken from sleep. So let everything that has breath praise Me, their King and Lord. My child, I am truly honored to hear from you this morning. It is a day of new beginnings. We will help you get through days when you are tired, sick, or unproductive. Through the healing power of the Holy Spirit, I am touching your body and making you whole again. No sickness, disease, or doctor's diagnosis can prevent you from living out your dreams.

I am healing and restoring you to the way you were originally created. Believe Me for the impossible. As you step out in faith, you will perform miracles that move mountains. Even if you have a mustard seed-sized faith, only believe. Jesus healed everyone who exercised their faith and declared that He was Lord over sickness, disease, and any bad report. Your faith will make you whole and deliver healing of your physical, mental, or spiritual conditions.

Scriptures
Psalm 150:5-6; Matthew 4:23, 9:35, 17:20;
Luke 17:6; Mark 5:36; Hebrews 11:6

Breakthrough Prayer

When my body is stricken with illness and disease, You heal me, Father. You will not allow me to die but heal and restore my life. It is Your will that I live an abundant life free of the bondage of sin. I know there are consequences to sin. Release me from any sin that the evil one sends into my life. Demolish demonic strongholds and addictions. Holy Spirit, make me whole—mind, body, and spirit. In Jesus' name, I pray. Amen.

BREAKING CURSES AND RELEASING BLESSINGS
Day 18

I decree and release myself from any sicknesses, diseases, illnesses, aches, pains, and anything contrary to Your will, Father God.

I destroy and break any heredity conditions, respiratory issues, heart problems, and cardiovascular pains in Jesus' name.

I decree and release myself from any generational curses on my father's and mother's sides.

I destroy and break any unhealthy appetites, desires, and hungers that bring diseases and sicknesses, in Jesus' name.

I decree and declare that the blood of Jesus Christ heals me when I am sick.

I destroy and curse at the root, and break myself free from any recurring sickness or disease that tries to come back stronger, in Jesus' name.

I decree and ask God to release healing angels in my life.

I destroy and break any airborne disease or bacteria.

Day 19

Psalm 103:12

*He has removed our sins as far from
us as the east is from the west.*

God Forgives and Forgets Your Sins

Forgive yourself from the pain of the past. Forgive yourself, My child, and understand that you cannot undo the past. Forgive yourself and others who hurt you deeply. Forgive yourself for allowing circumstances to make you bitter, not better. Forgive yourself for not finishing what you started. Forgive yourself today for what happened yesterday. Make it a point to forgive until you are no longer held captive and you are truly free. Do not let unforgiveness destroy your destiny or your relationships. Have you ever been wronged? Yes, you have, and you have in the past wronged someone. However, I require My children to forgive others as I forgive My own. Unforgiveness is the enemy's prime tactic against you to keep you from breaking through. Unforgiveness binds the offense to your heart and ensures you never forget what happened. As I forgive and forget, so shall you, My child.

That is why I plead with you, My child, to release anything from your past or present that has you holding on to resentment, pain, distrust, or anger. When you forgive, you release others from the debts incurred when they hurt you. Choosing to put others' sins behind you is a challenge. It is much easier to fixate and replay offenses than forgive. Decide to cleanse yourself from any unrighteousness that would keep you or others from walking under an open heaven. As you forgive yourself, I remember these sins no more—removing them as far as the east is from the west. That is My everlasting promise to you. It is My unbreakable covenant with you.

Scriptures
MATTHEW 6:14-15; MARK 11:26; EPHESIANS 4:32;
COLOSSIANS 3:13; HEBREWS 8:12; ISAIAH 43:25

Breakthrough Prayer

Father, there are days when I am just not on top of things. Some days are more stressful than others. Help me to rest in Your sovereign presence. I don't want stress to dictate my days or cause me to fall into sin. When I am consumed with worry and carry the cares of this world on my shoulders, I know that I can boldly come to You, Father, with a repentant heart. Your Word declares that my sins are forgiven and You will no longer remember my sins. In Jesus' name. Amen.

BREAKING CURSES AND RELEASING BLESSINGS
Day 19

I release myself from any harbored resentment that closes open heavens over my life.

I destroy and break myself free from any strains and pains caused by past hurts, in Jesus' name.

I release myself from any sin that I have not confessed and that I took ownership of.

I destroy and break any shame and guilt caused by any action done by others or myself, in Jesus' name.

I decree and release the sword of the Lord against Leviathan and the spirit of pride (see Isa. 27:1).

I destroy and break pride, haughtiness, rudeness, arrogance, vanity, conceit, indignity, judgment, criticism, pessimism, and scrutinizing spirits in Jesus' name.

I decree and release the two-edged sword to execute the judgment written (see Ps. 149:6, 9).

I destroy and break the spirit of hate, strife, and anger that will cause unforgiveness, in Jesus' name.

I decree and release the sword of the Lord out of Your mouth against the enemy as I declare Your Word, Father God (see Rev. 19:15).

Day 20

Psalm 107:9

For he satisfies the thirsty and fills
the hungry with good things.

God Satisfies Your Thirst, Relieves Your Hunger

Keep your head up! Do not let what has happened erode your confidence. You are a mighty gate, an everlasting door that will usher in My glory. Know, My child, that the King of glory comes into your life to fight for you when you're under attack and feed you when you're hungry. You may ask, "Who is this King of glory?" It is Me—the Lord who is strong and mighty. I AM the One who is valiant in any battle that you may face. When you are in trouble, you can call on the Lord of hosts. Know that the King of glory will come to your aid. It is My desire and longing to shower good gifts on those who belong to Me.

The benefits of My kingdom are available to all who seek Me first and My will. Then everything else will be freely given to you. Get ready to be satisfied with joy, peace, and prosperity. Our desire is to reveal honor, love, reverence, and worship to you. Did you know that I am a jealous God? My love for you is extravagant and beyond measure. Let My River of love refresh you and carry you to your purpose in Me.

Scriptures
Psalm 24:7, 9; Matthew 6:8, 33;
Exodus 20:4-5, 34:12-14; James 1:17, 4:5-10

Breakthrough Prayer

Change my appetite, Father, to consume what You want me to consume. Fill me up to overflowing. Refresh my weary soul with Your Spirit. Pour out Your anointing upon me so I may dream dreams and see visions. Stir up a holy hunger, a constant craving for more of You. In Jesus' name, I pray. Amen.

BREAKING CURSES AND RELEASING BLESSINGS

Day 20

I decree and release the thirst and hunger of the Lord to accomplish the impossible in my life.

I destroy and break myself free from every negative energy and agency of satan in Jesus' name.

I decree and release upon myself, my family, and those I relate with the grace to break glass ceilings and brass walls.

I destroy and break the walls of Jericho—fall flat in Jesus' name.

I decree and release the voice of the Lord to trump the voice of the enemy.

I destroy and break the will of the devil and loose the will of the Lord in Jesus' name.

I decree and release myself from every bond of satan.

I destroy, renounce, and break all ungodly anger, and I give no place to the devil in my life in Jesus' name (see Eph. 4:27).

I remove and break every satanic seat and synagogue from my city and nation (see Rev. 2:13; 3:9).

I destroy and break any injustice, demonic tactic, or instigation to frustrate my season of blessings.

Day 21

Psalm 109:31

*For he stands beside the needy, ready to save
them from those who condemn them.*

God Stands for the Righteous

Know, My child, that there is no condemnation for those who
are in Christ Jesus. You are Mine. I do not saddle you with heavy
burdens of guilt. I will deliver you repeatedly from the spirit of
condemnation. I stand side by side with you. I have sent the Holy
Spirit—the Comforter, Counselor, Consultant—to empower *you*
to become more like Jesus. Each day, know that you are anointed
and appointed to bring a revolution to the status quo of life and
your generation. You are marked with greatness.

When you pray and I am silent, it may seem that I have totally
forgotten your needs. Not true. They are on my checklist. As you
work with Me and not against Me, things will flow to you. There
are those who may condemn, ridicule, tease, or even laugh at you.
I will deliver you from these negative attitudes. When times are
bad, just remember that My purposes are often birthed through
struggle and sometimes painful places. People may say "no" to you,
but I have come today to say "yes" to your desires and dreams.

Scriptures
Romans 3:4, 8:1; John 14:26, 16:13;
1 John 2:27; Colossians 3:2; Matthew 5:37

Breakthrough Prayer

Father, You stand by those You love. Help me to stand in faith, believing the Word of God will work in my life as I continue to believe in Your promises. I will not put my trust in my own knowledge or information but in Your covenant. In Jesus' name, I pray. Amen.

BREAKING CURSES AND RELEASING BLESSINGS

Day 21

I decree and release the righteousness of the Lord in my life.

I destroy and break the spirit of lack, poverty, and debt in Jesus' name.

I decree and release the favor of God that will cause me to be exalted in the timing of God and in His righteousness.

I destroy and break any sign of wickedness and evil in Jesus' name.

I decree and release the fire of God that will spark personal revival and spiritual transformation.

I destroy and break the spirit of competition and false labor in Jesus' name.

I decree and release the fire of God to burn up the idols in my city, territory, region, and nation (see Deut. 7:5).

I destroy and break the spirit of racism, discrimination, bias, favoritism, and hatred within my border and sphere of activity in Jesus' name.

I decree and release the power of the Holy Spirit to resist the devil and he will flee (see James 4:7).

I destroy, bind, and cast down the queen of heaven spirit and break her allegiance (see Jer. 44:17).

I decree and release that God will raise up righteous leaders in everyscity, righteous leaders in government, and righteous representatives in every church.

I destroy, bind, and break the power of Jezebel, Ahab's queen, and her witchcraft agenda that attacks the righteous moves of the Spirit and the prophetic, in Jesus' name.

Day 22

Psalm 111:5

He gives food to those who fear him; he always remembers his covenant.

God Remembers His Covenant

Good morning, My *anointed* one. While you were asleep, I was thinking about My covenant with you, and how much we have accomplished together thus far. I understand what is stirring in your heart. Your dreams will happen as you depend on Me and My provision. Allow and trust Me to empower you to achieve the greater things in Me. I am going to remove every blockage devised by the enemy. Know this day, My child, that I will take care of each and every need.

When Elijah went to the brook of Cherith to drink, I sent ravens to feed him breakfast and lunch. Elijah had to trust by faith that I would supernaturally supply his needs during an economic drought. You may feel at times that your brook has run dry, but know I have another plan in another place of provision for you. In the midst of a drought, I can bring the rain necessary to quench your thirst. Drink from Me and you'll never thirst again. You will not die of thirst or starvation. I am Jehovah-Jireh, the Lord who provides.

Scriptures
1 John 2:27; Psalm 105:15;
1 Kings 17:3-6, 18:44; John 4:13-14; Luke 1:17

Breakthrough Prayer

Moses, Joshua, and David are poignant examples of walking in Your purpose in their generation. Anoint me with this same ability and grace to obey Your Word and will. Renew my mind and strength so I remain focused on Your promises to provide my daily provisions. Thank You for keeping Your Word and Your covenant concerning my worth and wellbeing. In Jesus' name. Amen.

BREAKING CURSES AND RELEASING BLESSINGS
Day 22

I decree and release upon my family, relationships, and myself the covenant promises of the Lord.

I destroy and break spirits of deception, lies, forgery, misrepresentation, misinterpretation, assumption, and gossip that come to discredit and devalue my purpose, in Jesus' name.

I destroy, bind, and cast down every false goddess, idol, or deity that would operate against my life, family, ministry, church, marriage, children, city, or state, in Jesus' name.

I destroy, bind, and break every queen spirit that operates through a false feminist movement in Jesus' name.

I decree the power of unity and oneness will be released in my life.

I destroy, cast down, bind, and break every spirit of seduction, scandal or perversion that would operate through queen spirits in my life, ministry, family, church, city, territory, business, workplace, and region, in Jesus' name.

I decree and release the spirit of truth that will expose all falseness, falsehood, false teaching, teachers, and doctrines of men and devils in Jesus' name.

I destroy every crown that is upon every head of the queen spirit—be bound by angels with chains, gagged, and dragged, in Jesus' name (see Ezek. 21:26).

Day 23

Psalm 112:6-7

Such people will not be overcome by evil.
Those who are righteous will be long
remembered. They do not fear bad news; they
confidently trust the Lord to care for them.

God Invites You to Totally Trust Him

I know that you hear and see bad news daily, but, My child, these things will not deflate your spirit. As you put your trust in My protection and love for you, I will ensure that you will not be in harm's way. There are those who try unsuccessfully to overcome evil on their own. There are those who allow sin and evil to consume them to the point they lose their power over temptation, ungodly desire, and wrongdoing. Pray to overcome evil. Partner with My sovereign power and faithfulness to bring deliverance and salvation to souls held captive and living in darkness.

For I have given you overcoming power and authority through the Holy Spirit. I have transferred you from the kingdom of darkness into the kingdom of My marvelous Light. You have been redeemed by My power. Jesus came to liberate you from the old, sinful nature and brought you into a wonderful state of freedom and love. As you continue to mature in the knowledge of My dear Son, Jesus, your perspective will change. You will not live to die but die to self and live as Christ Jesus lives within you. The spirit of fear is broken. Now you can move into a realm of faith. Your name will be remembered because you are faithful to Me and to your calling.

Scriptures

1 Peter 2:8-10; Philippians 1:21;
2 Timothy 1:7; Luke 18:27; Matthew 19:26

Breakthrough Prayer

Your Gospel is the Good News. I want to hear Your voice about matters concerning me. Protect me from wicked plots and evil spirits assigned as "destiny assassins" in my life. Mark these assassins in the heavenly realm and prevent them from interrupting my spiritual rhythm. There's no foe that can ignore Your lion's roar. A day is coming when every knee will bow and every tongue confess that Jesus is Lord. I will not permit the adversary to sway me from Your truth and trust.

BREAKING CURSES AND RELEASING BLESSINGS
Day 23

I decree and declare that I will trust in the Lord with all my heart and lean not on my own understanding.

I destroy and break the spirit of codependence upon men that comes to control or manipulate me, in Jesus' name.

I decree and release to myself the assurance and confidence in who I am and my calling.

I destroy and break every relationship that had a hidden agenda or purpose, in Jesus' name.

I decree and release upon my life the power to acquire, attract, and get wealth.

I destroy, break, and bind the demonic principalities and powers operating in systems in my city and command that they will be removed, bound, and gagged from this territory in Jesus' name (see Eph. 6:12).

I destroy and break the powers of demonic princes and ask You, Father, to send Your warrior angels to demolish their purpose against me in Jesus' name.

Day 24

Psalm 113:7-9

He lifts the poor from the dust and the needy from the garbage dump. He sets them among princes, even the princes of his own people! He gives the childless woman a family, making her a happy mother. Praise the Lord!

God Will Bring You Out of Obscurity

Whenever you think all hope is gone, think again. Understand, My child, that I will not leave you hopeless or helpless. There are those who feel nobody understands them. You know what it is like to feel invisible or voiceless. I love to hear you speak and express your feelings. My child, there is nothing wrong about being yourself. This is how I made you and I love you just the way you are. I will break you out of obscurity and bring you into divine visibility because of your humility. As you take the low road and not the back roads as a shortcut I will then take you to the highway and freeway of blessings, favor, and honor.

You are My treasure, not an accident or a throwaway. You have so much to offer. I am jealous over My children because they possess tremendous value. I have set you apart to live as kings and queens in the earth. I will seat you in the presence of royalty. Get ready to be now positioned in the presence of people who have influence and power to get things done. Know that I will transform your dry season to a time of fruitfulness. Believe that I am your Provider. I will bless you and make you prosperous in all of your ways.

Scriptures
John 14:18; Psalm 56:6, 139:14; Genesis 22:12-14; Matthew 6:10, 25-34; James 1:5

Breakthrough Prayer

When I feel guilty about doing something that displeases You, I thank You for not judging me harshly but righteously. You have given me a revelation about atonement. You dust me off and clean me up so that I am whole again. I have committed myself to Your Word, which through Your authority releases healing into my body, mind, spirit, and soul. In Jesus' name, I pray. Amen.

BREAKING CURSES AND RELEASING BLESSINGS

Day 24

I decree and release the strength of an ox to break through in times of hardship.

I destroy and break myself free from every bondage, demonic roadblock, and detour in Jesus' name.

I decree myself coming out of hiding or obscurity.

I destroy and break the fear of men in Jesus' name.

I decree and release the boldness of the Lord to speak truth in season and out of season.

I destroy and break every yoke from off of my neck, and I burst all the bonds in Jesus' name (see Jer. 30:8).

I decree and release the visibility of the Holy Spirit in His right timing and season.

I destroy and break the spirit of ungodly isolation in Jesus' name.

I release myself from oppression, depression, stress, and timidity.

I destroy and break the arms of wickedness that try to come within my walls (see Ps. 10:5).

I release myself from any old covenant, agreement, or promise established out of ignorance.

I destroy, crush, and break in pieces the oppressor in Jesus' name (see Ps. 72:4).

Day 25

Psalm 115:11

All you who fear the Lord, trust the Lord!
He is your helper and your shield.

God Prospers Those Who Obey Him

Make righteous decisions today. The ways of the wicked will not prosper. The ways of the righteous will be blessed. I will cause everything you touch to turn gold—profitable and successful. Know, My child, that the fear of the Lord is the beginning of knowledge. As you trust in your King, understand that all your desires will be taken care of and you will not want for anything. For I not only desire for your bank account to prosper but also your soul. I am your Shield and your Buckler. When the enemy pursues you and wants to discredit you, know that I am in pursuit of him and will stop him in his tracks. He will not have access to your destiny and purpose because I am Sovereign and the One who holds all things.

No one can stop what I have anointed. Nothing can hinder what I have approved. No one can deny what I have appointed. It will take tenacity and obedience to push back the enemy. People will enter into your life who will attempt to manipulate and control your decisions. Be watchful and pray. For prayer releases My protection and blessings into your life and those close to you. You asked Me to separate your supporters from adversaries. Your opponents will be replaced with those who support your cause. Look for opportunities to bless those who curse you, pray for those who use you, and love those who hate you.

Scriptures

Psalm 18:2, 111:10; Proverbs 1:7, 9:10;
Matthew 14:38; Luke 21:36; 1 Thessalonians 5:16-18

Breakthrough Prayer

The wicked one arrives at the most inopportune times to challenge my Christian walk. He has no power over me. I belong to You, Father. Now is the time for me to close those doors, portals, and gates that I opened in ignorance or unwisely. Hand me the master key that keeps the doors locked, portals shut, and gates closed. You are my Helper during difficult times and tough decisions. You are the Gate that gives me total access and liberty to enter in and out of Your majestic presence. In Jesus' name I pray. Amen.

BREAKING CURSES AND RELEASING BLESSINGS
Day 25

I decree and release upon myself the financial breakthrough and miracles that are held up in the heavenlies.

I destroy and break the spirit of the beggar and the spirit of usury in Jesus' name.

I decree and release the ability to apply the wisdom of God as He instructs me by His Spirit daily.

I destroy and break spirits of disobedience, insanity, and rebellion in Jesus' name.

I decree and release the spirit of obedience, sobriety, sanity, and cooperation with the Holy Spirit.

I destroy and break pride, haughtiness, and conceit in Jesus' name.

I decree and declare that my sphere of authority is enlarging and sphere of activity is increasing as I trust in the Lord.

I destroy and break every wall erected by the enemy against my life in Jesus' name (see Ezek. 13:14).

I decree and release the gifts of the Spirit to bless others.

I destroy and break every altar erected and built by the enemy against my life, family, church, city, region, and nation, in Jesus' name (see Hos. 10:2)

I decree and release the true altars of the Lord that will release the glory of God.

I destroy and break every demonic covenant made by my ancestors in Jesus' name.

Day 26

Psalm 116:1-2

I love the Lord because he hears my voice and my prayer for mercy. Because he bends down to listen, I will pray as long as I have breath!

God Lends His Ear If You Will Listen

I will extend mercy to those who show mercy to others. I love to hear your prayers and that you are concerned about your life and others. You are not selfish; you think about Me as well. I am happy when you pray about gaining more wisdom, understanding, love, and favor. I love when you pray about spiritual things and bringing others into My presence. I love to hear you pray for your loved ones, finances, dreams, goals, and vision. In addition, I love when you contend for miracles and expect My hand to move in your life.

I love demonstrating My faithfulness and love to you. This is My covenant to you. We don't have a one-way relationship. You truly love Me and acknowledge Me openly. You are open about our relationship and testify in the way you walk with Me. As you speak to Me, I am willing to listen. Know that I am always listening and willing to respond to you.

Scriptures
Romans 9:15, 18; Exodus 33:19;
Acts 17:11; John 6:38

Breakthrough Prayer

Your power makes me ready to enjoy Your presence. Your Holy Spirit also equips me to meet every challenge. You bend Your ear to attend to my request. I thank You, Father, that I don't feel disconnected from You. When I call, You always answer. I can confidently move forward with my daily tasks in Your strength and power. In Jesus' name. Amen.

BREAKING CURSES AND RELEASING BLESSINGS
Day 26

I decree and declare that my ear gates are open to the frequency and sound of Heaven.

I destroy and break the deaf and dumb spirit in Jesus' name.

I decree and release confusion against every satanic and demonic conspiracy against my life, church, family, ministry, territory, city, and nation in Jesus' name.

I destroy and break spiritual dullness of hearing in Jesus' name.

I decree the secret counsel of the evil one or wicked be turned into foolishness.

I destroy and break every satanic sound, voice, or work in Jesus' name,

I decree and release every plan, plot, and strategy of hell is exposed, destroyed, and brought to light.

I destroy and break every demonic cycle of debt, depression, oppression, control, and sickness in Jesus' name.

I decree and release the whirlwind to scatter those who would unjustly conspire against my church, family, ministry, city, nation, and my life.

I destroy and expose every net that the enemy has set up; they will fall into their own destructive plans against me, in Jesus' name.

Day 27

Psalm 116:3-4

Death wrapped its ropes around me; the terrors of the grave overtook me. I saw only trouble and sorrow. Then I called on the name of the Lord: "Please, Lord, save me!"

God Will Deliver You from Death

Life may seem unpredictable. Your destiny may seem farfetched. Know that I have everything under control and hold your future in My hands. Death is not the conclusion of your destiny. Death has no control or power over you. I sent My Son, Jesus, to conqueror death and now the grave has lost its sting. No longer is death a thought but life is in Me. There are times you have inquired about the purpose of living; other times, you have felt empty.

Today, I will restore, revive, reconcile, and release you into what you were born to do. Know that I will save those who call upon My name. I will not walk out on you, turn My back on you or deceive you. Experiencing losses are part of life and can happen to every great leader. I've been teaching you endurance and preparing you for greater things. You have been training for reigning in the Holy Spirit.

Scriptures
REVELATION 1:18; 2 CORINTHIANS 5:17; GALATIANS 2:20; COLOSSIANS 3:1-4

Breakthrough Prayer

The spirit of death will not harass me. Guard my heart from any intrusion from the evil one. Death seeks to hang me in its noose, but Jesus cut the cords that would have strangled me and unraveled my dreams. The grave is summoning me, but Jesus came that I might have life and live freely and fully. In Jesus' name, I pray. Amen.

BREAKING CURSES AND RELEASING BLESSINGS
Day 27

I release myself from any attachments or spirits of the dead in Jesus' name.

I free and break myself from any individuals who died before they were able to forgive me of an offense, and I forgive, free and loose them from any offense done to me by them, in Jesus' name.

I release myself from any demonic word curses spoken directly or indirectly to bring spiritual or natural death and unproductivity.

I decree and release the sword of the Lord against Leviathan and the spirit of pride (see Isa. 27:1).

I destroy and break the spirit of pride, haughtiness, and conceit in Jesus' name.

I decree and release the spirit of life, seed of resurrection, and power of germination.

I destroy and break the spirit of murder, death, rage, anger, lunacy, and schizophrenia in Jesus' name.

I decree and release the peace of God that surpasses my understanding.

I destroy and break every demonic plan against me and I declare that they are turned back and brought to confusion in Jesus' name.

I decree and release myself from every ungodly object, item, and contract or will associated with the dead or deceased.

I destroy and break every bad encounter that brings about bitterness or resentment in Jesus' name.

Day 28

Psalm 116:5-6

*How kind the Lord is! How good he is!
So merciful, this God of ours! The Lord
protects those of childlike faith; I was
facing death, and he saved me.*

God Loves Childlike Faith

Pressure does not come to break you but to get you to your breakthrough. Stay flexible through the authority of the Holy Spirit. There are those who want you to bend or even break under pressure. I AM extending my loving-kindness and favor to you. Job prayed for his friends instead of agreeing with his wife's suggestion to curse Me and die. He understood the principle of acknowledging his Provider.

Prayer does not just change one thing; it changes everything and anyone, My child. As you pray for My kingdom in the earth and for generational blessings, I will download daily strategies and release impartation that will lead you to your promised land. Let Me keep you in perfect peace as your mind is fixed on Me. I watch over and protect those who come to Me with a childlike faith—innocent, pure, and humble and expectant.

Scriptures
Luke 4:18-19; Matthew 18:2-4; Luke 1:37;
Acts 16:25-34; Psalm 24:4, 51:10

Breakthrough Prayer

The enemy falsely accuses and slanders the saints of the Most High God. None of his tactics are justified. Through Christ Jesus, I am justified by faith. Father, there is no condemnation in You. The wicked one pushes for my conviction for my sins. In an earthly court, this would mean punishment—a maximum penalty or death sentence. Jesus paid it all for me. In Jesus' name, I pray. Amen.

BREAKING CURSES AND RELEASING BLESSINGS

Day 28

I decree and release upon myself the childlike faith to do the impossible.

I destroy and break the spirit of control that would operate from those in authority, in Jesus' name.

I release the love of Christ and decree that His agenda is exalted in my life.

I destroy and break every demonic reinforcement and confederacy against my life, ministry, family, church, city, business, and relationships in Jesus' name.

I decree and release myself from any demonic blockage, barriers, parameters, and fences of the enemy to hinder and frustrate the will and plans of God for my life, ministry, family, church, business, city, and territory, in Jesus' name.

I destroy and break the spirit of cunning and thievery in Jesus' name.

I decree and release the blessing of the Lord that makes me rich and adds no sorrow.

I destroy, break, and quench fiery darts the enemy sends my way with the shield of faith (see Eph. 6:6).

I release myself from any spirit that comes to take advantage or capitalize on my ignorance and innocence, in Jesus' name.

I destroy and break every torch the enemy would use against my family, ministry, business, church, property, life, and relationships.

I release myself from the spirit of loneliness and the orphan spirit.

I destroy and break the spirits of perversion, immorality, incest, and rape that come toward the young, elderly, and innocent in my city, region, state, and territory, in Jesus' name.

Day 29

Psalm 116:7-9

Let my soul be at rest again, for the Lord has been good to me. He has saved me from death, my eyes from tears, my feet from stumbling. And so I walk in the Lord's presence as I live here on earth!

God Is Good to His Children

"Why me?" you have asked. I have heard you say that time and time again, My child. My response remains the same: "Why not you?" In My eyes, you are not a follower but a leader cut from a different cloth. I have a special work only you can do. When you feel like you are walking on a balancing beam and think you will lose your footing, know there is a safety net ready to break your fall. You will not crack under pressure or miss out on your destiny. Often you wonder why bad things happen to good people. Look up and see things from Heaven's perspective. Get ready; I am loosing the spirit of breakthrough over unexpected circumstances.

My child, you will not fall victim to injustice. I will keep you aligned perfectly to My will. Stay the course. Do not quit. You are too close to the finish line. If you feel burned out, I will give you rest and dry every tear from your eyes. Instead of falling into traps planned for your demise, you will leap over them and lead others to Me. You are My secret agent who will bring many souls to glory. You may have felt mistreated, but I am good to My children.

Scriptures
Psalm 62:5-12, 121:7; Proverbs 4:23;
1 Peter 5:8; Jeremiah 39:18

Breakthrough Prayer

Father, I ask that You keep me afloat despite the raging waters that come to throw me overboard and instill fear. I do not want to drown in the cares of this world. Show me how to navigate through the currents. Impart faith and courage into my heart and liberate me from the spirit of fear. You are my Lifeline in turbulent times. You are my ever-present Helper in my time of need. I rejoice because Jesus is the Rescuer of my soul. In Jesus' name, I pray. Amen.

BREAKING CURSES AND RELEASING BLESSINGS

Day 29

I decree and declare that I am the righteousness of Christ.

I destroy and break every spirit of malice and cruelty in Jesus' name.

I release the rain of heaven that delivers blessing now.

I destroy and break every diabolical system that opposes my time of advancement, in Jesus' name.

I decree and declare that my future and times are in God's hands.

I destroy and break every pinnacle of pride and false glory that satan wants to deceive me with in Jesus' name,

I decree and release fresh manna, revelation, and insight from Heaven.

I destroy and break sluggishness, laziness, contentment, and boredom in Jesus' name.

I release myself from false expectations from those in authority, family members, and those I have working relationships with.

I destroy and break the spirit of blackmail, charm, craftiness, and sneakiness from others.

I destroy and release Your hot thunderbolts against the enemies of my destiny in the spirit in my city, region, and territory in Jesus' name.

Day 30

Psalm 118:14-16

The Lord is my strength and my song; he has given me victory. Songs of joy and victory are sung in the camp of the godly. The strong right arm of the Lord has done glorious things! The strong right arm of the Lord is raised in triumph. The strong right arm of the Lord has done glorious things!

God Sings Your Love Song

Did you know that My Son, Jesus, forever lives to make intercession for you? Intercessory prayers don't just move mountains, they remove hardness from hearts. Know My transforming power will usher change into your life. I desire to hear a new song—a war anthem signaling impending victory. All will stand in amazement when I perform My supernatural acts. Let Me exercise My power in your life. As enemy resistance arises, My strong arms are safely holding you.

I've put the enemy on notice that you belong to Me. The enemy stands on the front lines ready to pursue you when you let your guard down. We are sending Our army of angels to strong-arm and defeat your adversaries. We will put your enemies on notice. There is no contest. Evil is no match for your King and Lord God. You are My loving child! Exercise your spiritual muscles through life's trials and triumphs. Faith is often tested when you are in your weakest moment. Know that you are an overcomer in Christ Jesus!

Scriptures

Psalm 89:13; 2 Corinthians 1:8, 12:9-10;
1 Samuel 30:8; Exodus 18:23; James 1:12

Breakthrough Prayer

You are my love song. When I sing to You, I am strengthened. In Your presence, I am free to be me. You are my joy, peace, and happiness. Align my spirit with Yours so that I am in total harmony with You. I do not want to be off-key or in discord. When I sing in the Spirit, I sing with my understanding. Holy Spirit, as I yield myself to You, birth new songs within me. In Jesus' name. Amen.

BREAKING CURSES AND RELEASING BLESSINGS
Day 30

I decree and release the songs, lyrics, beats, harmonies, and sounds from Heaven in my worship time with the Father.

I destroy and break the spirit of confusion, weariness, and fatigue in my life in Jesus' name,

I release myself from legalistic worship and religious restraints that hinder the move of the Spirit.

I destroy and break old wineskin patterns and the spirit of conformity in Jesus' name.

I decree and release the prophetic songs that will cause the dew of Heaven to drop in my city, church, ministry, and territory.

I destroy and break every serpent spirit and voice of deception in my ear.

I decree and declare that the bars of my gates are now strong in my city; by the grace of God I will advance the kingdom of God (see Ps. 147:13).

I destroy and break every political agenda that does not serve the purpose of the kingdom of God my life in Jesus' name.

Day 31

Psalm 119:105

*Your word is a lamp to guide my
feet and a light for my path.*

God's Word Becomes Your Flashlight

Good morning, My powerful one. I want you to know that you are loved with My everlasting love. I watch over you as an eagle watches over its eaglets. Let Me provide for your daily needs. I know what you need even before you start to pray. Don't sweat the small stuff, My child. Things should not become heavy burdens or responsibilities. Let us not concentrate on what you cannot control. Let go of worry. Keep your eyes on the prize—your dream, goal, and vision.

Turn your attention to what pleases Us—loving yourself and others. There are three things that you must possess—faith, hope, and the greatest of them all is love. Did you know that I am Love? I loved you so much that I sent Jesus to sacrifice Himself because My heart is for the world that I created. I have plans for your future. Walk hand in hand with Me and allow My Word to illuminate your calling and destiny the same way a flashlight floods a walkway with its brilliantly bright light.

Scriptures
1 Corinthians 10:13; Matthew 6:8, 34; John 3:16, 4:24;
1 John 4:8, 16; Luke 12:32; Deuteronomy 32:11

Breakthrough Prayer

Father, Your Word is the handbook for living my life. It gives me clear direction no matter how intimidating things seem. Holy Spirit, You keep my feet pointed in the right direction. Train me to discern Your leading. Open my ears to hear what Your Spirit is whispering to me every step of the way. In Jesus' name. Amen.

BREAKING CURSES AND RELEASING BLESSINGS
Day 31

I decree and release the lamp of the Lord upon my feet and light upon my pathway.

I destroy and break the spirit of darkness and ignorance in Jesus' name.

I decree and release the spirit of wisdom, guidance, and directives of the Lord to sustain me.

I destroy and break the spirit that comes to cause spiritual blindness in Jesus' name.

I decree and release Holy Spirit fire that will ignite revival in my life, family, church, city, state, region, and territory.

I destroy and break the spirit of dullness, disorder, and confusion in Jesus' name,

I decree and release upon myself the divine exposure that is needed to catapult me into another season.

I destroy and break every demonic exposure and opportunity sent to set me up for failure, in Jesus' name.

I decree and release the secrets and plans of the Lord over my life prophetically (see Amos 3:7-8).

I destroy and break all curses by agents of satan spoken against my life in secret or in darkness, in Jesus' name (see Ps. 10:7).

I decree and declare that I am released out of the midst of every cauldron.

I destroy and break every demonic assignment sent to bring death to my vision and purpose, in Jesus' name.

Day 32

Psalm 119:114

You are my refuge and my shield;
your word is my source of hope.

God Is the Source of Hope

I want you to know that life is not ruled by the number of breaths you inhale but by the number of times that cause you to exhale. I have come to cause you to live longer, become healthier, and experience a joyful life in the Holy Spirit. There are times when you will hurt, cry, and be upset. From these life lessons, I want you to lend your to strength to someone else who may be going through the same pain, hurt, or misunderstanding that you faced. There are those who feel desperate and contemplate ending their lives because of overwhelming demands that the world places on them or they place on themselves.

You will be a shining light that dispels the darkness of their thoughts and helps them see their worth of living. Their lives—and yours—are important. Choose life over death. Many people would be brokenhearted and truly miss you. Life is so precious and you are precious to Me. As you rely on the source of the Word, you will begin to realize that it will guide you through every season of decision. Staying in My Word positions you to make the right decision at the right time.

Scriptures
Romans 14:17; John 10:10;
1 Corinthians 8:6; John 1:4, 5:26

Breakthrough Prayer

Father, I understand that You are the only source of hope, love, and peace. Your peace is remarkable and can calm any traumatic situation. Jesus is the Hope of the world. Without Him I am lost and buried in sin. Your love vindicates me and presents me faultless before my adversaries and haters. Help me to recognize individuals You've called me to work with so that I will accomplish Your will. In Jesus' name. Amen.

BREAKING CURSES AND RELEASING BLESSINGS
Day 32

I destroy and break the demonic manipulation that casts spells to bewitch me and those in the Body of Christ, in Jesus' name,

I decree the hedges of protection by God over my life, family, city, church, ministry, business, marriage, relationships, and properties.

I destroy and break every false hope, false expectation, false dream, false prophecy, and false vision.

I decree and release great grace upon my life to do the impossible in Christ for my generation.

I destroy and break the demonic container housing or hosting my destiny; it will collide with the rock of ages now in Jesus' name.

I decree and release the blessings of the Lord that will bring balance, sustainability, and expansion.

I destroy and break every demonic cage restricting my life and those who I come in covenant with in Jesus' name.

Day 33

Psalm 119:165-168

Those who love your instructions have great peace and do not stumble. I long for your rescue, Lord, so I have obeyed your commands. I have obeyed your laws, for I love them very much. Yes, I obey your commandments and laws because you know everything I do.

God Instructs the Teachable

Listen to My voice this day as I lead you with new instructions. As you follow My leading by My Spirit, you will not find confusion but peace. You will not fall or stumble. Like a lifeguard saving a swimmer, I want to rescue you. Obey My Word and follow My lead. For Jesus My beloved Son is *the Way*, *the Truth*, and *the Life*. When you feel that you have lost your way, I will make a way for you. When you feel as if you are walking in error, I will reveal truth to you. When you feel as if you are facing death, I will give you life.

It is because of My love for you that I'm in covenant with you. Obey My commandments by the Holy Spirit and I will direct you path. I desire to ignite the fire again within you and spark that passion to run this race with ease. Trust My laws that I have written upon your heart and will constantly remind you. I will not leave you stranded on the side of the road or hitchhiking.

Scriptures
Deuteronomy 28:1; Jeremiah 7:23;
John 14:16, 15:10; 1 Corinthians 14:33

Breakthrough Prayer

I know, Father, it is Your will for me to succeed. You desire the best for me and only the best. You have put the seed of impossibility in me through the Holy Spirit. I want to be an obedient child. I know You do not want me to breach Your covenant or break Your Word. Show me areas where I have erected idols in my life so I can destroy them. I will exalt You as the only true and living God. In Jesus' name. Amen.

BREAKING CURSES AND RELEASING BLESSINGS

Day 33

I decree and release the spirit of humility on my life.

I destroy and break the unteachable spirit and know-it-all mentality in Jesus' name.

I decree and release the power of conviction by the Holy Spirit whenever I am walking in the wrong way.

I destroy and break every snare of the enemy that comes in opportune times in my life, in Jesus' name.

I decree and release the culture and principles of the kingdom over my life, ministry, business, church, family, and leaders I relate with.

I destroy and break every demonic, invisible line that has been drawn around my life, and they are abolished now in Jesus' name.

I decree and release the boundaries of the Lord over my life, family, city, church, ministry, business, marriage, relationships, and properties.

I destroy and break every demonic safe, vault, and storage that tries to lock out my destiny, in Jesus' name.

I decree and release the keys of the kingdom of Heaven to unlock my destiny and purpose in Christ.

I destroy and break the spirit of self-entitlement that seeks attention in Jesus' name.

Day 34

Psalm 121:1-2

*I look up to the mountains—does my help
come from there? My help comes from the
Lord, who made heaven and earth!*

God Sends Help Wherever You Are

My mighty warrior, know there is no situation or problem too
large or enemy too fierce for Me to handle. Look for Me to flatten
every mountain standing in your way. There is no pain too deep
that I cannot ease it. Know, My beloved, that I will soon exchange
the pain you're feeling for unspeakable joy. A new season is approaching. Stop comparing yourself to others. What I have prepared for you is just for you. It is more than your eyes have seen,
your ears have heard, or has ever crossed your mind. No one could
ever imagine what we will achieve together.

There are secrets that I will soon reveal to you. After all, who
would you rather have fighting on your side—the Maker of the
heavens and earth or mere men? Yes, I will continue to send men
to deliver blessings to your door. Remember, we raise up kings and
queens and dethrone them. Trust in the King who knows your
past, present, and future.

Scriptures
2 Corinthians 10:12-16; Amos 3:7;
1 Corinthians 2:9; Exodus 15:3

Breakthrough Prayer

I am faced with daily decisions and responsibilities that can be overwhelming. Life can be like a traffic jam. Long waits and detours can lead to frustration and road rage. Holy Spirit, engulf me in Your peace and patience. Help me relax and not be in a rush. Impossible circumstances become nothing in Your eyes, Father. In Jesus' name. Amen.

BREAKING CURSES AND RELEASING BLESSINGS
Day 34

I decree and release the protection and guardianship of the Lord upon everything that I am involved in.

I destroy and break every mental cage that I have established in my own mind that limits me, in Jesus' name.

I decree and release the spirit of creativity to stretch and launch out into deeper things in the Spirit.

I destroy and break every cage of restrictions and non-achievement working against me.

I decree and release upon my life the power of influence to change the world for Christ.

I destroy and break every evil power that is sitting on my breakthrough, in Jesus' name.

I decree and release upon myself the fire of God that will propel me forward to accomplish great things in Him.

I destroy and break the spirit of jealousy working against my destiny.

I decree and release the spirit of love that will change the most callous of hearts.

I destroy and break every curse of automatic failures, disappointments, and let downs in Jesus' name.

Day 35

Psalm 121:3

He will not let you stumble; the one who
watches over you will not slumber.

God Won't Let You Fall

I am overly protective of you, My child. While you sleep, I watch over you both day and night. Your every step is predestined by Me. I know the way that will lead you in the right direction. There are many roadways but only one that takes you to Me. My child, would you rather take a broad and crowded highway or a narrow road that few follow? I have placed destiny markers to guide your way.

When you are uncertain about your calling, you may think you misunderstood Me. Be confident you have been called for such a time as this. You were not born by accident but for a divine purpose. I do not make mistakes, nor do I create things without giving them a God-given purpose. Every day, life puts what you have learned to the test. As you lean on the Holy Spirit, you will begin acing life's tests.

Scriptures
Job 23:10; Psalm 138:8;
Romans 8:29, 12:2; John 14:26

Breakthrough Prayer

Heavenly Father, You never slumber. You will not allow me to stumble because You have planted my feet on a firm foundation—Your Word. I can rest assured because You keep watch over me day and night. Thank You for spiritually equipping me with Your whole armor to battle against unseen forces. In Jesus' name. Amen.

BREAKING CURSES AND RELEASE BLESSINGS
Day 35

I decree and release the wings of an eagle in the spirit that I might mount up on and soar beyond personal obstacles.

I destroy and break every evil eye looking, monitoring, influencing, and surveying my destiny, in Jesus' name.

I decree and release the eyes of the Lord to influence and direct my every move by the Holy Spirit.

I destroy and break every spirit that comes to bring unhappiness into my life over the years; be arrested and destroyed now in Jesus' name.

I decree and release great and healthy relationships that will bring happiness, peace, and joy in the Holy Spirit.

I destroy and break the demonic artillery fired and sent against my life; it will backfire with fire, shame, and destruction in Jesus' name.

I destroy and break every ancestral and generational curse that has carried over from my family from generation to generation; stop now in Jesus' name.

I decree and release renewal, revival, restoration, reconstruction in every area that the enemy attacked and seized.

I destroy, annul, and break all curses of destruction and death against my life, family, and bloodline in Jesus' name.

Day 36

Psalm 121:7-8

The Lord keeps you from all harm and watches
over your life. The Lord keeps watch over you
as you come and go, both now and forever.

God Is Your Keeper

Begin your morning with Me. I want you to know that I will keep you from danger. When you feel like you do not know if you are coming or going, simply be still and know that I am your God. I want to speak to you. I love talking with My children, but I don't always communicate the same way with you. I long to speak with you about things that may not make sense to you now but will later. Know that I will not leave you in darkness but illuminate your prayer needs.

It brings Me great joy knowing that you know why you are here. Continue walking in your heavenly career and earthly assignment. Even as I have given the first Adam a place of rulership and dominion, he was able to multiply himself. I placed man in My Garden of Eden to manage and subdue the earth. It is My vision to see you establish your own Eden in the earth. You are called to rule as king-priests in the earth and have dominion in the Holy Spirit.

Scriptures
Genesis 1:28, 2:15; 1 Peter 2:9;
Proverbs 3:5; Psalm 115:16

Breakthrough Prayer

Let me receive Your peace and love today, Father. Impart prophetic revelation so that I can see things with my spiritual eyes. Deliver me from the demonic agenda of the evil one. For those who are oppressed, I pray for freedom by the power of Your Word. You have given me power over all dark forces. Shine the light of Your justice and expose all hidden agendas. In Jesus' name, I pray. Amen.

BREAKING CURSES AND RELEASING BLESSINGS

Day 36

I decree and release the treasure of God in my life, family, church, ministry, and business.

I destroy, evict, and break the spirit of pride that would open the door for death and destruction, in Jesus' name (see Prov. 16:18).

I decree and release the boldness of the Lord like a lion to obtain victory.

I destroy and break the spirit of poverty and destruction that comes in times when I advance.

I decree and release the faith required to move mountains.

I destroy and break every influence that is assigned against my destiny in Jesus' name.

I decree that I can possess what I prophesy by the Holy Spirit.

I destroy and break unhealthy patterns in my life that serve no purpose of spiritual growth and personal enrichment.

I decree and declare that no weapon formed against me shall prosper and every tongue that rises against me in judgment I condemn (see Isa. 54:17).

I decree and release the favor of the Lord upon my life because of my obedience to God's Word.

I decree and release uncommon favor and unrestricted blessings of God in every area of my life.

I destroy and break every word curse sent to irritate, frustrate, and aggravate my prophetic destiny, in Jesus' name.

Day 37

Psalm 124:8

*Our help is from the Lord, who
made heaven and earth.*

God Moves Heaven and Earth for You

My child, I have heard your complaints and pleading. Know that I love to hear what is on your mind so we can work things out. Let Me impart strength and wisdom you need. The Holy Spirit will guide you to all truth and revelation of Jesus Christ. You will receive Heaven's support and reinforcement when you find yourself at a dead end. As Moses approached the Red Sea, I opened it up like a bridge and allowed My people to cross over on dry land. The Promised Land is waiting for you.

The enemy is chasing you. He wants the Red Sea to become your graveyard. Put the enemy in his place. I have given you the power and authority to defeat demonic spirits that come to terrorize and torment you. No longer are you enslaved by the enemy's ways. My covenant keeper, Christ, lives on the inside of you.

Scriptures

ROMANS 1:1; HABAKKUK 3:19; EPHESIANS 6:10;
JOHN 16:13; PSALM 105:8; EXODUS 14

Breakthrough Prayer

I cannot imagine not having You in my life. You are the Creator of Heaven and earth. There is nothing too difficult for You. It is my desire to walk in Your will and see Your covenant promises manifest in my life. Holy Spirit, comfort me through seasons of confusion. Father, answer my heart's cry to love myself and others as You love me. In Jesus' name. Amen.

BREAKING CURSES AND RELEASING BLESSINGS
Day 37

I decree and release the floodgates of Heaven to invest in my spiritual calling.

I destroy and break the work of satan that comes to steal, kill, and destroy me physically, spiritually, economically, personally, socially, and mentally.

I decree and declare that I am established in righteousness and oppression is far from me in Jesus' name (see Isa. 54:14).

I destroy and break every glass ceiling, demonic oversight, or illegal covering that is in authority.

I decree and release healthy, productive, godly, and honest covenant relationships in my life.

I decree and release upon my life the vision of God that brings clarity, understanding, and insight.

I destroy and break any undercover and scheming spirit sent to bring shame, in Jesus' name.

I destroy and break the stronghold grip of Jezebel, Herod, Pharaoh, and every demonic prince that is sent against my destiny and calling in the earth.

I decree and release the sword of the Spirit, which is the Word of God, to use it to overcome the already defeated enemy of my destiny (see Eph. 6:17; Col 2:15).

I destroy and break every demonic whisper of influence that comes to deceive and manipulate, in Jesus' name.

Day 38

Psalm 125:1

*Those who trust in the Lord are as
secure as Mount Zion; they will not be
defeated but will endure forever.*

God's Love Endures Forever

When you place total reliance and faith in Me, you will be like a strong mountain that cannot be destroyed. You will be like a fortified city that cannot be shaken. You will not be overtaken even when you feel you are at the end of your rope. My child, you will not lose breath but get your second wind. Get ready for a time of transition. The enemy tries to knock the very breath out of you with his hardest blow. I will swoop down like a raging mother eagle and rip him apart. I guard and protect My beloved.

Ask for My assistance. You will be like a military armory that is fully loaded with the weaponry of heaven. Do not be afraid to step out of the boat into the sea of faith. Peter wavered in his decision to trust Jesus when he was called out of his comfort zone. I will cause your faith to arise so that you can do supernatural things. Understand that faith without works is lifeless. Give your faith an assignment, My child. Your faith matures as you move forward in obedience.

Scriptures
1 Corinthians 10:13; Isaiah 52:12, 58:8;
James 1:6, 2:26; 1 Samuel 15:22

Breakthrough Prayer

Help me to follow You by faith and not by what I can see in the natural. I have withstood many loses. Father, release what You have for me. I repent for wandering away in disobedience to Your teaching. I want to become more proactive in following Your orders. In Jesus' name. Amen.

BREAKING CURSES AND RELEASING BLESSINGS
Day 38

I decree and release the Father's love that will bring healing, restoration, reconciliation, and peace.

I destroy and break demonic persuasions, attractions, deceptions, manipulations, and gains in Jesus' name.

I decree and release the spirit of compassion to understand and to relate to the most difficult people.

I destroy and break every ungodly appetite that warrants unnecessary sickness, attacks, and attention.

I decree and release the ability to be social and interpersonal when need be.

I destroy and break the spirit of confusion, instability, and insanity in Jesus' name.

I decree and release upon myself the wisdom of the Lord to obtain wealth.

I destroy and break the lies of the enemy sent to bring a negative impact or influence against my ministry, life, family, and work.

I decree and release the ability to discern the times that I am in and make right decisions.

I destroy and break every false perception of me by men in Jesus' name.

Day 39

Psalm 126:5-6

*Those who plant in tears will harvest with shouts
of joy. They weep as they go to plant their seed,
but they sing as they return with the harvest.*

God Trades Your Sorrow for Joy

My child, I want you to understand that what you have en-
dured has not been in vain. Everything has a purpose and a reason.
Nothing happens by accident. What you sow in tears, you'll soon
see turn around. Rejoice, for your harvest is coming. I have an
inheritance that I will release to you, and I will cause you to enjoy
the best of your increase. You will come into a season of heavenly
access, My child. What you pray today, you will see manifested
tomorrow.

As you experience a deeper walk with me, I will share deeper
secrets with you. I will not have you walking in ignorance. I will
not have you praying and missing your mark. This morning, press
toward the mark of the high calling in Christ Jesus. You will never
miss when you are securely anchored in Him. Hardships make
you stronger and empower you to overcome any situation that
arises unexpectedly. My child, I want you to dream bigger and live
better! The best is yet to come. Go get your harvest!

Scriptures
Psalm 23:2, 126:5-6; Philippians 3:14;
Job 22:28; Romans 12:15-16

Breakthrough Prayer

My heart feels as if it has been ripped out of my chest. I have shed many tears and taken lots of loses along this journey. Those very dear to my heart have been snatched away. I have been left alone. Why does the pain hurt that much? Why, Father, am I labeled different, weird, strange, and even unique? I do not understand myself, but You call me normal and Your special one. What I sow in tears, I will reap in joy. In Jesus' name. Amen.

BREAKING CURSES AND RELEASING BLESSINGS

Day 39

I decree and release the joy of the Lord upon my life, family, church, ministry, and business.

I destroy and break disorder, contention, anger, and confusion that comes to steal my inner joy, in Jesus' name.

I decree and release upon myself the overcoming strength needed to press past barriers of fear.

I destroy and break the system of control and oppression that is an enemy of my destiny.

I decree and release the power to mobilization that will empower and influence the next generation.

I destroy and break the spirit of stagnation in Jesus' name.

I decree and release the endurance needed to persevere in the midst of demonic opposition.

I destroy and break every demonic spirit and influence coming to hinder godly success in my life.

I decree and release spiritual, economic, financial, career, marital, domestic, mental, prophetic, and medical breakthroughs in my life in Jesus' name.

I decree and release the spoilers to come upon Babylon and destroy her in the name of Jesus.

I destroy and break satanic palaces, bunkers, and headquarters of darkness in Jesus' name (see Amos 3:11).

Day 40

Psalm 130:4

*But you offer forgiveness, that we
might learn to fear you.*

God Loves When You Forgive Others

Forgive and forget, My child. Unforgiveness brings "dis-ease" to the soul. It is the enemy's tactic to cause your prayers to go unanswered by Me. He knows how We feel about harboring unforgiveness in your heart. Liberate yourself! Words have power. There is life and death in the power of your tongue. You can set wildfires when you use your tongue like a match, igniting a fire that is hard to extinguish. Be quick to hear and slow to speak. Do not allow offense to cause you to miss the dreams that I have for you. I desire to break any strongholds of offense that keep you from realizing your destiny.

For even as I am a forgiving and loving Father, Jesus became the example of love and forgiveness even to the point of death. He is your role model of what love looks like. His love was not selfish but sacrificial. You love Me and your heart cries out to Me without an agenda. I love you on purpose just as it was My love on purpose that My Son Jesus sacrificed His own life just for *you*. Jesus is not only the prime example of love but also a symbol of forgiveness and My redemptive power. I gave up My Son because I love you. He gave up His life because We love you immensely and eternally.

Scriptures

James 1:19, 3:8; Proverbs 14:29, 18:19; John 3:16;
Matthew 18:15-17; Romans 12:1

Breakthrough Prayer

Father, I am determined to press daily into Your presence and into Your kingdom. In Your presence, I can examine myself and learn to forgive myself from past regrets, hurts, pains, and unforgiveness. Through Your eyes of forgiveness, I can forgive others and myself as Your Word commands. In Jesus' name, I pray. Amen.

BREAKING CURSES AND RELEASING BLESSINGS

Day 40

I free and release myself from any unresolved issue, circumstance, problem, grudge, and ought against someone.

I destroy and break barriers set against me by those in authority who doesn't see my full potential, gift, calling, and heart, in Jesus' name.

I repent, free, and release myself from any sins unknown or forgotten, in Jesus' name.

I destroy and break myself free from any systems and methods of men that produce the wisdom of men and not the wisdom of God.

I decree and release wealth and riches are in my house and my righteousness will last forever (see Ps. 112:3).

I destroy and break the spirit of poverty and lack away from my house in Jesus' name; unrighteousness is not my portion.

I decree and release the joy of the Lord, which shall empower and strengthen me and those I pray for daily.

I destroy and break myself free from chains of bondage that come to stop the process of maturation and development.

I decree and declare that I dwell in the secret place of the Most High and I abide under the shadow of the Almighty (see Ps. 91:1).

I destroy and break roots of unforgiveness or bitterness that close my spiritual Heaven and blessing, in Jesus' name.

Day 41

Psalm 135:14

*For the Lord will give justice to his people
and have compassion on his servants.*

God Extends Justice to His People

Be patient with Me, My child. I am teaching you to not only experience life but enjoy it the fullest. When you are wrong, I will correct you and give you clarity. When you are right, I will praise you and give you greater understanding. Even when people mistreat you and falsely accuse you of wrongdoing, I will clear your name and redeem your reputation. I will vindicate you and give you justice. Know, My child, that I am causing you to break free from any illegal soul ties that keep you bound to others.

Avoid verbal and contractual agreements with anyone outside of our covenant. I desire for you to connect with those who keep their word and walk in integrity. For I am a God who honors My Word above My name, and know, My child, that I will honor and esteem you above the heathen of this world. I am not one who will lie or a son of man who needs to repent. My compassion toward you is unconditional and covenant based. Let us converse daily and map out your destiny. I show favor to those I love and have chosen.

Scriptures
Matthew 5:11; Isaiah 43:1; Hebrews 4:12;
Acts 4:32; Deuteronomy 7:9

Breakthrough Prayer

Father, I thank You for defending me no matter what and covering me with Your love. There are those who will come with a plan to expose me. Please open my spiritual eyes so I am not blindsided. Show me a preview of what You want to show me in the Spirit. Burden my heart to pray for injustices. I want to see Your kingdom's "law and order" released in my life. In Jesus' name. Amen.

BREAKING CURSES AND RELEASING BLESSINGS

Day 41

I decree and release the justice and favor of the kingdom of God over my life.

I destroy and break any misfortune, mishaps, mistakes, and miscommunications sent to sabotage, in Jesus' name.

I decree and release favorable judgment against me.

I destroy and break every illegal judgment and attack against my life, character, and integrity.

I decree the spirit of prosperity that will release that which is owed to me and back pay.

I destroy and break every civil lawsuit and every unlawful criminal prosecution against me that is unjust, in Jesus' name.

I decree and release unprecedented favor upon my life, family, ministry, church, business, and relationships in Jesus' name.

I destroy and break every stronghold and pillar that stands in my way.

I decree and release the Samson anointing and strength to break through any resistance.

I destroy and break spirit of deception that comes to rob me of my natural and spiritual inheritance, in Jesus' name.

Day 42

Psalm 138:3

*As soon as I pray, you answer me; you
encourage me by giving me strength.*

God Encourages and Strengthens You

Good morning, My warrior! I heard your prayers asking for My
assistance. Simply be still and listen as I speak to your inner man.
Listen to the small still voice within, the inner witness inside you.
For it is Jesus' voice whispering to your spirit man, calling you to
a higher place in Us. We desire the best for you and nothing less. I
want you to see yourself doing great things in Me. I cast off every
limitation and remove any ungodly appetites that might trip you
up. For the enemy wants you to eat the desires and cares of this
world. You are in the world but not called to conform to its patterns.

You are peculiar on purpose and never meant to conform to this
world. I have called you out to call you into bringing revolutionary change. People will misinterpret your willingness to be different as rebellious, but you are not. There is a revolutionary living
inside of you. I have marked you with the strength and creativity
to make waves that will have a lasting impact and will usher in
change. I hear your prayers and I am committed to answering
them. You are on My priority list. I will not postpone talking with
you but will respond as soon as the time is right.

Scriptures
Matthew 17:1-9; 1 Kings 19:11-13; Psalm 20:2

Breakthrough Prayer

Share Your thoughts with me about what You need me to change. I do not want to make any excuses or blame shift. What areas do You need me to work on? I am happy to know that I am not praying in vain, and my prayers are answered in a timely manner, not by my clock but on Your heavenly timetable. Your infinite wisdom and thoughts are beyond what I can comprehend. Thank You, Father, for being You. In Jesus' name. Amen.

BREAKING CURSES AND RELEASING BLESSINGS
Day 42

I decree and release the spirit of liberty upon my life that will take me to new places (see 2 Cor. 3:17).

I destroy and break the spirit of depression that comes with too many responsibilities that aren't mine, in Jesus' name.

I decree and declare that the gift of prophecy will be stirred up on the inside of me to encourage, exhort, and edify the Body of Christ.

I destroy and break the spirit of loneliness and rejection by those who are authority figures and my peers.

I decree and release the spirit of joy, peace, and righteousness in the Holy Spirit over my life, family, church, ministry, business, and city.

I destroy and break discouraging news that will alter my mood and day, in Jesus' name.

I decree and declare that I am walking in my wealthy place and will be a blessing in Jesus' name.

I destroy and break every negative pattern and distractions that comes in my path.

I release myself from all religious yokes, rules, mindsets, and bondages (see 2 Cor. 4:5).

I destroy and break old ways, mindsets, paradigms, concepts, ideas, and thoughts that are not in line with the will of God on my life, in Jesus' name.

Day 43

Psalm 138:7-8

Though I am surrounded by troubles, you will protect me from the anger of my enemies. You reach out your hand, and the power of your right hand saves me. The Lord will work out his plans for my life—for your faithful love, O Lord, endures forever. Don't abandon me, for you made me.

God Has a Special Plan for You

My child, while you were in your mother's womb I chose you. I have established your calling and set you apart for a special work and assignment. We have already drawn up a blueprint for your life. Yes, trouble will come. Fight against being swallowed by fear. I will break the fear factor that wants to pollute your mind. I will lift the cloudiness from your mind and fill up the light of faith. The enemy is angry and anxious to see your downfall, but this day I have made your face like flint. Despite your adversary's evil intentions, I will help you maneuver around them and show you the way of escape.

Let My mighty hand of power protect you from the hungry wolves bent on discrediting your name and detaining your destiny. They will not tear apart My dreams for you. My plans and purposes for your life are simple—to save you time and time again from the enemy's frivolous lies and schemes. I know how to work out what may seem to you unsalvageable. I am faithful to perform My Word, so have faith in what I can do. Only believe and you will witness My miraculous power working in your life. Do not give up on Me. I will never give up on you because I have given up My Son who sacrificed His life for you and all humanity.

Scriptures

ACTS 20:29; LUKE 11:8; 2 THESSALONIANS 1:6; 1
THESSALONIANS 5:24; DEUTERONOMY 7:9

Breakthrough Prayer

Teach me to be slow to anger. I don't want to let anyone or anything frustrate my day. Give me Your peace that goes beyond anything I can imagine! I believe You will work out my daily schedule, and I will follow wherever You lead. In Jesus' name. Amen.

BREAKING CURSES AND RELEASING BLESSINGS

Day 43

I decree and release upon my life the blueprint of my destiny to be fulfilled in my lifetime.

I destroy and break every disturbing, destructive, and disruptive spirit in Jesus' name.

I decree and release upon myself a new awareness to walk in new levels of accountability in the truth of God's Word (see James 1:22).

I destroy and break every assignment to devalue me, my family, my church, my ministry, my business, my friends, and any associations.

I decree and release Holy Spirit utterance to speak with boldness, and the mystery of the gospel will be made known unto me (see Eph. 6:19-20).

I destroy and break all diabolical plots, plans, and tactics against my life, body, and family, in Jesus' name,

I decree and declare that God's will toward me is not of evil but of an expected future.

I destroy, break, and shatter the gates of hades or hell that come to prevail against me.

I decree and declare that God will be a wall of fire around me and His glory will be in the midst.

I destroy and break every work of darkness over my city, state, region, community, and country in Jesus' name.

Day 44

Psalm 139:3

You see me when I travel and when I rest at home. You know everything I do.

God Knows Your Destiny

Live in the moment and enjoy life. It all begins with right thinking. You are what you speak and you are what you imagine. The power of the spoken word is a creative force that can change your atmosphere. I know where you are when you find yourself lost in your decisions. I know when you are in a place of restlessness. I want to order your steps according to your faith. I know everything about you and your day. Nothing is hidden from Me.

Equip yourself. Stay focused. Finish what you start. Surround yourself with people who value your time as well as their own. Persevere like the ant. Your sacrifices will not go unnoticed or unrewarded. Get ready to do things that you have never done before. Determine each day to set a personal record.

Scriptures
ROMANS 4:17; ECCLESIASTES 1:4-11; LUKE 22:42;
MATTHEW 11:28-30; PROVERBS 27:17

Breakthrough Prayer

You know everything about me. You created me, Father. There is nothing I can hide from You. There is no secret that I can hide from You. The Holy Spirit is the Investigator and will convict me of wrongdoing. I am delighted to know that You observe when I leave and when I return. You watch over me when I lie down and awaken. Is anything too hard for You? In Jesus' name. Amen.

BREAKING CURSES AND RELEASING BLESSINGS
Day 44

I decree and release the revelation knowledge and wisdom upon my life to accomplish what I was called to do.

I destroy and break every enemy and spirit of divination that comes to stop me from pursuing my destiny, in Jesus' name.

I decree and release the power of vision to see with precision, accuracy, and clarity my gifts, calling, and assignment in the earth.

I destroy and break the spirit of dullness of hearing, sight, and understanding.

I decree and release the ability to advance the purposes of God; every place the soles of my feet shall tread, God has given it to me (see Josh. 1:3).

I destroy and break all diabolical plots, plans, and tactics against my life, body, and family in Jesus' name.

I decree and declare that my destiny is accelerated as I come into agreement with it and God's Word.

I destroy and break the powers of witchcraft prayers and prophecies that are sent to deceive me.

I decree and declare that my feet are planted in the Word of God and I shall not be moved.

I destroy and dismantle every substitute, demonic replacement, and spirit sent illegally, in Jesus' name.

Day 45

Psalm 139:4-5

*You know what I am going to say even before I
say it, Lord. You go before me and follow me.
You place your hand of blessing on my head.*

God Knows Your Life's Plan

Be slow to speak, and open to hearing what I have to say to you this morning. I know what you are thinking before you ever form thoughts in your mind. I know what you're going to say before others hear it. I know what you will do before others see it. I am very much aware of your beginning and ending. Know that a disciplined mind creates a disciplined life. I want to change your worldview and how you view yourself. The thoughts I have toward you are not evil ones but good ones that will bring you to your divine destiny. But know that there are enemies of your destiny that delight in your failure.

I come to break through the enemy lines and bring you to your expected end. With David I burst through like a water to defeat the enemy; so shall I be with you as the Lord of the Breakthrough. Others' failures should not shape you. I am molding and refining you into a perfect vessel and My representative in the earth. Refuse negativity and embrace My positive power. Do not allow past victories to become ancient history; instead, use them as a catalyst for future triumphs. Walk alongside Me—not stepping outside of My divine plan. Take My hand and I will lead you to a place of blessings.

Scriptures
Philippians 3:13-14; Matthew 4:19;
Isaiah 43:18; Psalm 139:2-4; Job 14:5

Breakthrough Prayer

Before a single word comes out of my mouth, You know what I am about to say. You can read my mind before I even formulate my thoughts. There is nothing discreet about You. I come boldly to Your throne of grace with a humble heart. If I need deliverance in my life, show me those actions, attitudes, and behaviors that I need to change. Anoint my head with the oil of Your Spirit. Bless me as I travel. In Jesus' name. Amen.

BREAKING CURSES AND RELEASING BLESSINGS
Day 45

I decree and declare my set time of favor will not be delayed but released now in Jesus' name.

I destroy and break the work of satan who fights against me and the will of God on my life.

I decree and declare that the purpose and plan of God over my life is sharp and I am running with it.

I destroy and break ungodly oaths, negotiations, and contracts that are not a part of my purpose in God.

I decree and release the blessings of God that will cause residual income and wealth streams to support my vision.

I destroy and break any illegal alliance, mafia spirit, or gang activity that would attach itself to me, my family, my business, and my friends, in Jesus' name.

I decree and declare that my destiny and purpose is secure in the hands of the Lord.

I destroy and break all powers of hell that are released from the grave, hades, the underworld, the four regions under the earth, and Sheol, in Jesus' name.

I decree and declare that my God-given assignment is marked for success.

I destroy and break the shackles of debt and poverty off my life and everything I am called to build in Jesus' name.

Day 46

Psalm 139:7-10

I can never escape from your Spirit! I can never get away from your presence! If I go up to heaven, you are there; if I go down to the grave, you are there. If I ride the wings of the morning, if I dwell by the farthest oceans, even there your hand will guide me, and your strength will support me.

God Is Your Biggest Fan

My Spirit will not depart from you as you maintain your faith in Us. My presence will not leave you; My Spirit will quicken anything that is lifeless. Know that you will remain physically and spiritually healthy instead of flatlining on life's operating table. I am healing you and touching those tender places of your heart. My child, I can lend a helping hand because My arms are not too short to reach you. Wherever you go, We are watching over you.

Know that I am everywhere. If you go to the heavens, I am there. If you make your place in the grave, I am there. If you ride the wings of the morning or go to the deepest part of the earth, I am there too. I am your Provider and your Guide. Jesus paid it all in advance so you are not expected to pay for your sins. Do not run the risk of jeopardizing anything that has been placed in your hands. Seize every moment as if it is your last. Raise high the bar of expectation. Every time you jump up to reach it, you will touch the ceiling of personal success.

Scriptures

Genesis 6:3; Isaiah 41:10; Exodus 40;
Romans 8:11; Psalm 139:8

Breakthrough Prayer

You are Omnipresence. I can never run away where You cannot find me. I cannot do anything without You knowing about it. I cannot go a day without communing with You. I cannot escape Your abiding and comforting presence. I know that I am safe in You when I need an escape from the busyness of life. In Jesus' name. Amen.

BREAKING CURSES AND RELEASING BLESSINGS
Day 46

I decree and declare that I will stay in God's presence for protection, comfort, and direction in Jesus' name.

I destroy and break the spirit of fatigue that tries to weigh me down or cripple me.

I decree and release the anointing of the Holy Spirit that causes me to complete my assignment with a God ease.

I destroy and break anything that is not synchronized with the purpose of God on my life, family, marriage, children, friends, church, ministry, and city.

I decree and release the ability to be sensitive to the Holy Spirit's leading and walk in obedience.

I destroy and break every demonic sound and noise that comes to distract and cause deafness spiritually, in Jesus' name.

I decree and declare that my spirit man is being renewed and my soul awakened.

I destroy and break all powers that expand problems and pray they shall be paralyzed in Jesus' name.

Day 47

Psalm 139:13-14

You made all the delicate, inner parts of my body and knit me together in my mother's womb. Thank you for making me so wonderfully complex! Your workmanship is marvelous—how well I know it.

God Created You Inside Out

Life can be complex and difficult at times. It was not hard for Me to fashion you into who you are today. I enlisted your parents to create You, My masterpiece. When you were conceived, you displayed My workmanship. You are very delicate in every way. As you grew in your mother's womb over those many months, I was anticipating your arrival.

You are a miracle! You survived the beginning of your birthing process and are now moving toward realizing your full potential. You are a champion of champions. The very fact that you can think like a champion positions you to become one. Embrace who you are in this season and let people see the real you—no masks, no more walls, no pretense. Understand that there will never ever be someone like you in the earth. You have so much to deposit in the earth that will bless those who are heirs of your inheritance.

Scriptures

Psalm 139:13-14; Galatians 3:29;
Romans 8:17; Jeremiah 1:5

Breakthrough Prayer

I know becoming like Jesus requires personal sacrifices. I am willing to surrender and suffer much to carry Your magnificent glory on my life. If I suffer with Christ, I will reign with Him. You know my inward parts. You understand how everything functions and operates. You masterfully created me and took Your time shaping me into a vessel of honor. You are my Potter; I am Your clay. In Jesus' name, I pray. Amen.

BREAKING CURSES AND RELEASING BLESSINGS
Day 47

I decree and declare that I will discover the seed of greatness on the inside of me in Jesus' name.

I destroy and break seeds sown by the enemy of division, dissention, confusion, and disorder.

I decree and declare the ability to rediscover the treasures of God inside me and use them for His glory.

I destroy and break every ungodly and unhealthy covenant I might have been enticed to make, in Jesus' name.

I decree and declare that every aspect of my life will yield abundant and exponential blessings, harvest, and fruit.

I destroy and break every curse of modern-day Baalam or false prophetic voice against the will of God in my life in Jesus' name.

I decree and declare the anointing for creativity in my ministry, church, business, career, life, and family.

I destroy and break the power of the agent of debt in my life in Jesus' name.

I decree and declare divine wisdom and understanding that brings about success.

I destroy and break all lies of the adversary that say I cannot make it in this year, in Jesus' name.

Day 48

Psalm 139:16

You saw me before I was born. Every day of my life was recorded in your book. Every moment was laid out before a single day had passed.

God Holds Your Spiritual Birth Certificate

Count the cost of what you do. Plan well and learn to communicate. Your words and ideas can make you or break you. Trust in what I advise you. We counted the cost when We created you. We realized that you were created to be priceless and cannot be bought. I have recorded your every step. Your destiny is already settled. Be a faithful steward of your time and manage it well. The enemy will try to stop your spiritual clock and the special times and seasons that We have prepared for you.

We have determined what you would like, would become, and would do for Us. Know that your cooperation with the Holy Spirit's leading will only accelerate your time. I'd rather have you be early or on time than behind the times and stuck in an old season. There are people in your life who are not destined to follow you. Learn to invest wisely in your spirituality and time. You will gain value and a better return on everything you sow.

Scriptures
Isaiah 8:10, 57:14; Luke 14:28;
Romans 8:28; 2 Chronicles 15:7

Breakthrough Prayer

Before I was born, You had a plan for me. I was created from Your mind and DNA. I was the pattern etched into Your heart. It is Your desire that I become more like Jesus. Becoming more like Jesus means encountering trials and tribulations and adopting His nature and character to be Christ-like in the earth. I was created to represent Jesus who overcame the sins of the world. I am an overcomer in Him! In Jesus' name, I pray. Amen.

BREAKING CURSES AND RELEASING BLESSINGS

Day 48

I decree and declare that shattered dreams, hopes, and visions be revived in Jesus' name.

I destroy and break every spiritual rage sent in my life.

I decree and declare that I am walking in my ordained calling established by Heaven and godly leadership.

I destroy and break every trait of spiritual backwardness in Jesus' name.

I decree and declare that by faith Jesus will supply all my needs spiritually, physically, emotionally, mentally, and economically.

I destroy and reject any relationship that may drag me into ungodly habits, in Jesus' name.

I decree and declare that the power, glory, and the kingdom of the living God will come upon every aspect and sphere of my life.

I destroy and reject a life of strife and envy in Jesus' name

I decree and declare that I shall be blessed with supernatural favor and abundance that will bless generations to come.

Day 49

Psalm 139:17-18

How precious are your thoughts about me, O God. They cannot be numbered! I can't even count them; they outnumber the grains of sand! And when I wake up, you are still with me!

God's Thoughts about You Are Numerous

My love will never fail you even when you feel no one else loves you. Each day, I make it possible for you to see a new day of accomplishment. Ever feel that you have lost the battle or race you've been running? Know that My heart and thoughts about you are good. Imagine the number of grains of sand on a beautiful beach. That is how infinite My love and thoughts are for you, My child.

Ever been in love, My child? You cannot stop thinking about your loved one. That only begins to describe how extravagant My love is. You are always in My heart and on My mind. I want you to be love sick for Me. Be assured that I travel with you on this journey. This journey that you will take is life's journey to fulfill your prophetic destiny. But in the meantime I will navigate your every step and bring you to a place of awareness of the greatness that is lodged within you. My thoughts toward you are just that—they are centered and focused on your overall success!

Scriptures
Lamentations 3:22; Psalm 136;
1 Corinthians 9:24; Hebrews 12:1; 2 Chronicles 20:17

Breakthrough Prayer

Your thoughts concerning me are not negative but always positive. Your thoughts toward me are holy, loving, and pure. I know that You don't like some things I say or do, but You have faith in me and believe for the best. Your thoughts cannot be numbered. There are far too many to count. In Jesus' name. Amen.

BREAKING CURSES AND RELEASING BLESSINGS
Day 49

I decree and declare that all my lost and stolen finances be released and recovered in Jesus' name.

I destroy and break every negative thought about me, my family, and my relationships.

I decree and declare that Jesus is my strong tower; I run into Him and I am safe.

I destroy and oppose every power of darkness that opposes my restoration in this year.

I decree and declare that all my treasures that the enemy has stolen will be returned in full.

I destroy and reject any life of strife, resentment, bitterness, or unforgiveness in Jesus' name.

I decree and declare that I possess the spirit of watchfulness and spiritual alertness.

I destroy and reject a life of strife and envy in Jesus' name

I decree and declare that wisdom is my portion and understanding will help me walk in success that bring blessings.

I destroy and reject the sins of the mouth, sensual sins, hypocrisy, malice, strife, hatred, and verbal assaults against those in leadership, in Jesus' name.

Day 50

Psalm 140:12

But I know the Lord will help those they persecute; he will give justice to the poor.

God Defends the Persecuted

When you face persecution, refuse to shrink back or retreat. Stand on the promises in My Word. Persecution and oppression came to the children of Israel but could not break their spirits or dismantle their destiny. The Israelites received My Word, power and, provision when they desperately needed a sign through Moses. The Word delivered a nation out of slavery. One word from Me, My child, will not only liberate you from hidden bondages but those connected to you. I will rescue you when people persecute you.

I will fight for you and deliver justice just as I did for the Israelites. The more they faced persecution, the more they grew stronger. They matured and soon outnumbered the Egyptians. I will make a way of escape for you in the wilderness. I saw their afflictions and heard their cries. As I was with them, so will I be with you. Trust that I will provide an exit plan from your wilderness.

Scriptures
MATTHEW 5:11-12; LUKE 6:22;
1 CORINTHIANS 10:13; EXODUS 1:12-14

Breakthrough Prayer

Father, help me to wait on You. Provide discernment, through the Holy Spirit, that allows me to determine right from wrong. I have experienced personal persecution on all levels. It hurts my feelings when loved ones reject me for no reason. You attend to the needy in their time of needs. Thank You, righteous Judge, for being in my corner. In Jesus' name. Amen.

BREAKING CURSES AND RELEASING BLESSINGS
Day 50

I decree and declare that my ship will not sink due to sudden persecution by others, in Jesus' name.

I destroy and break tempest winds, storms, or hazardous weather patterns that come to bring destruction.

I decree and declare that there shall be an accelerating breakthrough on my way this day and year.

I destroy and bind all evil hosts that may want to gather against my progress and my family, in Jesus' name.

I decree and declare that no darkness shall come my way today and throughout this year.

I destroy, break, and reject satan's suggestion that I will not receive success this year, in Jesus' name.

I decree and declare that there shall not be any abandoned projects this year.

I destroy and reject every life-wasting and draining project and unnecessary burden in Jesus' name.

I decree and repossess supernatural financing to rebuild every broken place in my life.

I destroy and break every ungodly ambition and agenda in Jesus' name.

Day 51

Psalm 144:2

He is my loving ally and my fortress, my tower of safety, my rescuer. He is my shield, and I take refuge in him. He makes the nations submit to me.

God Will Make Nations Honor You

Capture the moment. Do you always take the road that I have mapped out for you? No, but My grace is sufficient. I am patient when you make a wrong decision. I know you are tempted to go your own way. Just as the heavens are higher than the earth, My ways and thoughts supersede yours. My plan for you reaches to the stars. I know your faults, failures, and fears. You aren't immune to failure. I have marked out your course, and often it will include failure. When you do things your own way without applying My precepts, failure is inevitable. However, even the most public failure can become the greatest victory in the hands of Christ.

At times, you may not make wise decisions regarding your life, finances, and relationships. I have given you the decision-making instead of letting someone else make decisions for you. Never give away your personal power. I will expose every diabolical cycle that attempts to rob you of your dignity, peace, joy, love, blessings, rest, success, and hope. Know that I am your loving Ally who will give your life stability and balance. When you lack strength, I will become your Fortress, your Tower of Power. To block the enemy's blows, let Me be your Shield and Buckler. I am your Refuge when you need to rejuvenate.

Scriptures

2 Corinthians 12:9; Psalm 18:2, 91:2; Deuteronomy 8:16

Breakthrough Prayer

You are my way maker. Your direction for my life is sure, unwavering, and just. I am not confused when led by Your Holy Spirit. Your Word ensures my feet stay on the narrow path. Sometimes, I second-guess myself. Thank You, Holy Spirit, for being the Witness who confirms my decisions line up with the Word. I chose to die to self and allow Christ to live in me—even if the company I keep does not agree with me. You are my Love Warrior. My battles belong to you. I pray this in Jesus' name. Amen.

BREAKING CURSES AND RELEASING BLESSINGS
Day 51

I decree and declare that people will give me my due honor, recognition, and award for my service.

I destroy and break off demonic chains that keep me bound to past exploits, defeats, success, and positions within the realms of darkness.

I decree and declare that myself and my family are victors and overcomers who will no longer be held back by the lies and torments of the past.

I decree and declare that I will walk under and open heaven, and dreams and visions shall be pour out by the Holy Spirit.

I destroy and break every pattern of unsuccessful goals, agendas, and objectives.

I decree and declare that I will no longer allow the past to hitch-hike, blackmail, and renege on me, nor will it cause me to go out of my way for it.

I destroy and break all ties with the past, its occupation in my thoughts, both conscious and subconscious, and I cut off all attachments and false identities resulting from the past and all it entailed, in Jesus' name.

I decree and declare that the works of my hands are blessed and I am compensated for my service fairly.

Day 52

Psalm 145:8-9

*The Lord is merciful and compassionate,
slow to get angry and filled with unfailing
love. The Lord is good to everyone. He
showers compassion on all his creation.*

God's Mercies Never End

Guard your heart, eyes, ears, and mouth from anything that disagrees with My desire for you. Season your words with My divine wisdom and knowledge. I will hand over the master key, which gives you access to doors of opportunity. My love, mercy, and compassion can change any condition even when people are unlovable, unmerciful, and cruel. I will show you a better way of handling the most unusual, unbearable, and unreasonable circumstances and situations.

Know that I reject pride and extend favor and grace to those who are humble. I am merciful and compassionate, My child. I have sent My Son, Jesus, as a man to undergo the same things you face. You want to live in a perfect world instead of this fallen world. Partner with the Holy Spirit's power and anointing to shift the atmosphere for the better.

Scriptures
PROVERBS 4:23; MATTHEW 5:5, 15:17-19;
COLOSSIANS 4:6; 1 CORINTHIANS 16:9; JAMES 4:6

Breakthrough Prayer

Father, help my family and friends understand why I choose to pursue You. Some question my commitment to You and it causes conflict. I am torn and frustrated with my loved ones, but I know You understand. Your love is unfailing and irresistible. You extend mercy to the merciful. In Jesus' name. Amen.

BREAKING CURSES AND RELEASING BLESSINGS
Day 52

I decree and release brand-new mercies daily upon my life, family, and those that I am connected to in Jesus' name.

I destroy and break every spirit that comes to cripple me, disable me, and harm me.

I decree and declare that I am redeemed from the curse of the law, sickness, poverty, and spiritual death (see Gal. 3:13).

I destroy and break the spirit of worrying, anxiety, and insomnia that causes me to stress out over what I don't know, in Jesus' name.

I decree and declare that there is extended mercy and favor upon my church, ministry, business, marriage, city, state, and region.

I destroy and break wasteful resources and agendas in Jesus' name.

I decree and declare that this year will be a year of surplus, more benefit, increase, and bonuses.

I destroy and break old cycles and release new cycles of blessings.

I decree and declare I will overcome all because greater is He that is in me than he that is in the world (see 1 John 4:4).

I destroy and break every plot sent against my life that will cause repeated mistakes in Jesus' name.

Day 53

Psalm 145:14-15

The Lord helps the fallen and lifts those bent beneath their loads. The eyes of all look to you in hope; you give them their food as they need it.

God Is Present for the Fallen

Good morning, My faithful one. You are a good soldier who has served through turbulent times. At times, the journey has been bumpy, but you have remained poised in spite of it all. Let go of stress and pressure. I can make your schedule and workload easier for you to bear. Look for Me, and you will surely find Me. Another precious promise: I will stay by your side whenever and wherever you are. You and I have a rich relationship. My goal is to aid souls who have fallen in battle. Grab hold of My hand when you are bruised, beaten, or wounded. Know that I will lift up your head when you are downcast. Turn over every burden that you have been shouldering alone to Me.

Yes, My child, I'm not finished with you. I am still maturing you. Keep in mind, My child, that increased anointing on your life means higher responsibility to come. I am preparing you to spark the next move that people have been waiting to see. As you point people to Me, they will look up to heavens and turn their lives over to Me. I will welcome them into My family and provide as faithfully as I have for you. Watch doubts dissolve and faith seeds sprout into oaks of righteousness. Those who seek covering under these mighty oaks will also find leaves of hope, joy, and peace.

Scriptures

PSALM 3:3; ROMANS 7:23; GENESIS 50:25; EXODUS 13:19; JOHN 15:2

Breakthrough Prayer

Gone are the heavy loads from my shoulders. I do not intend to bend or break under the weight of the world. Fill me with Your grace to tackle life's demands and deadlines. Lord, I look to You to renew my mind and restore my hope. In Jesus' name. Amen.

BREAKING CURSES AND RELEASING BLESSINGS

Day 53

I decree and declare I am delivered from the path and grips of the roaming lion in Jesus' name.

I destroy and break every hidden demonic device, trap, and invisible fence in the spirit.

I decree and declare my hand is upon the neck of the enemy, and he will not advance (see Gen. 49:8).

I destroy and break the patterns of failure and letdowns in Jesus' name.

I decree and declare that I will arise a good soldier and child of the Lord.

I destroy and break false friendships, acquaintances, comrades, associates, and partners in Jesus' name.

I decree and declare that I will be authentic and original to bless my generation.

I destroy and break the spirit of haughtiness and a lofty mentality that doesn't bring God glory.

I decree and declare that I tread upon serpents, scorpions, and over all the power of the enemy, and nothing shall by any means harm me (see Luke 10:19).

I destroy and break every spirit that comes into any natural database to bring error, in Jesus' name.

Day 54

Psalm 145:18-20

The Lord is close to all who call on him, yes, to all who call on him in truth. He grants the desires of those who fear him; he hears their cries for help and rescues them. The Lord protects all those who love him, but he destroys the wicked.

God Is Closer Than You Think

Get ready this morning for a greater release of My anointing. Get ready to depart the cave of Adullam, which has been your hiding place. I am removing every demonic stronghold and fortress that comes to weaken you. I am your refuge and your hiding place. Come out of that fortified cave of life and fight. I am going before you! Feel My presence and know My voice. For in Me I will become that place of healing, restoration, revitalization, and preparation for combat. You have been in training for reigning. I am positioning you for your next assignment. Know I will respond when you call on Me in truth.

When you walk with godly wisdom and reverential fear, I will grant the desires of your heart. Cry out to Me, your heavenly Father, the way a baby cries for help, comfort, or nourishment. Parents know immediately when their babies are ready to eat, burp, sleep, or cuddle. You are My baby. I know what you need and when you need it. Even though you are capable of making your own decisions, walk humbly and lean on Me for everything.

Scriptures
1 Samuel 22; Jeremiah 30:17;
Psalm 37:10, 94:14; Isaiah 49:15; Galatians 3:26

Breakthrough Prayer

Father, grant my prayer requests as I kneel before You in reverence and awe. Anoint me with the Spirit of Truth, and give me success in the midst of error. Thank You that You hear me when I cry. When I petition You today, I come before You with boldness and confidence. I know You will review or approve my request in accordance with Your Word and will. In Jesus' name, I pray. Amen.

BREAKING CURSES AND RELEASING BLESSINGS

Day 54

I decree and declare that the glory fires of God's presence will be demonstrated in my life in Jesus' name.

I destroy and break strange fire, false doctrines, and doctrines of devils that want to influence me.

I decree and declare the Lord will teach my hands to fight and my fingers to war.

I destroy and break low mentality or small-mindedness in Jesus' name.

I decree and declare that my life, family, friends, church, ministry, business, marriage, children, and divine connections are blessed with all spiritual blessings in heavenly places (see Eph. 1:3).

I destroy and break the false lenses and perceptions of Christ that come by false teaching of Jesus' life, death, burial, and resurrection, in Jesus' name.

I decree and declare that I am anointed by God through the Holy Spirit to preach, teach, heal, prophesy, cast out devils, evangelize, and raise the dead.

I destroy and break doctrines that produce fear, intimidation, and paranoia of death or dying, in Jesus' name.

I decree and declare that I have life in Christ and will have it more abundantly.

I destroy and break false teaching against the present-day prophetic, healing, and miracle ministry.

Day 55

Psalm 146:7-8

He gives justice to the oppressed and food to the hungry. The Lord frees the prisoners. The Lord opens the eyes of the blind. The Lord lifts up those who are weighed down. The Lord loves the godly.

God Extends Justice to the Oppressed

Just when you think you have reached your lowest point, I will supply extra horsepower for you to claim your victory. Get back in the race! It is not given to the swift or the strong but to those who do not give up. Arise and shine and know that My glory shall be risen upon you. I will break the spirit of fear that comes against your willingness to conqueror your giants and fears. Know that I am impossible and the God of miracles. I can create springs out of desert places. Arise and eat for the journey of destiny is approaching. You will break through. When you see the armies of Pharaoh pursuing you to entrap you, I will cause the spiritual Red Sea to split and become their gravesite.

When the enemy is coming against you like a flood, know, My child, that I will raise up a banner against them. Moreover, when you feel like you cannot go any further, I will feed you supernaturally to run to the finish line. I was the One who supernaturally gave Elijah remarkable speed to race past Ahab's chariot. Believe for the impossible and watch what I will do in and through you. When you feel that you have been oppressed, shake off everything weighing you down. Join forces with the righteous who stand before Me, and you will receive justice against the spirit of oppression.

Scriptures

Proverbs 21:31; Psalm 147:10; Job 39:19;
Isaiah 58:6; Nahum 1:13; 2 Kings 6:17-20

Breakthrough Prayer

Father, loose me from the spirit of entitlement and any claims that men have made. In the face of injustice, You deliver Your verdict and determine restitution. Tear down any strongholds that prevent me from operating in Your will. I expect good things to happen today. In Jesus' name. Amen.

BREAKING CURSES AND RELEASING BLESSINGS

Day 55

I decree and declare that I am totally liberated from the spirit of oppression in Jesus' name.

I decree and declare that I am victorious in Christ and it is expressed through the work that I am called to do.

I destroy and break every negative thoughts and assumptions in Jesus' name.

I decree and declare that I am the righteousness of Christ and the blessing of God is my portion.

I destroy and break idle words spoken out of ignorance, in Jesus' name.

I decree and declare that I am called to influence, change, and bring a revolution to my generation for Christ.

I destroy and break down word barriers, restrictions, and boundaries sent by those who are not faith builders.

I decree and declare I receive an abundance of grace, and the gift of righteousness reigns in my life through Christ Jesus (see Rom. 5:17).

Day 56

Psalm 146:9

The Lord protects the foreigners among us.
He cares for the orphans and widows, but
he frustrates the plans of the wicked.

God Cares for the Poor and Helpless

Good morning, My blessed one. There is no partiality when it comes to those I chose to bless and show favor. Great is My faithfulness and heart for the lost, brokenhearted, poor, and needy. Their needs are no surprise to Me. Moreover, if you let Me, I will take care of your needs. Do not let pride keep you from receiving all that I have stored up for you and your loved ones. I will not have you naïve about what is brewing in the enemy's camp.

Ever since you received the anointing of the Holy Spirit, your adversary is determined to distance you from My will. His intention is to frustrate you so you cannot clearly hear My directives for your life-path. My record of accomplishment speaks for itself. I have a history of frustrating opponents and disarming their wicked plots. I have not forgotten you, My child. I have not sidelined you. The battle has astounded you. I will revive you and your vision. I will protect those within your house, borders, and sphere of influence.

Scriptures
Luke 1:28; Psalm 34:18, 115:15, 138:7, 147:3;
Matthew 6:10; Hosea 6:2

Breakthrough Prayer

Frustrate the plans of the evil one. Cancel his assignment; his strategies are null and void. Father, You protect orphans and widows who are in need. You are a good Father who never abandons His children or ignores their requests. When my mother and father forsake me, You embrace me without reservation. You whisper in my right ear that all is well. Keep reassuring me that I have nothing to fear because You are near. In Jesus' name. Amen.

BREAKING CURSES AND RELEASING BLESSINGS

Day 56

I decree and declare that I will never be broke or live in a realm of poverty, in Jesus' name.

I destroy and break lack, debt, unsecured loans, and spirits of poverty.

I decree and declare God is now able to do exceedingly abundantly above all that I ask or imagine by the power that works in me (see Eph. 3:20).

I decree and declare that I am debt free and have excellent credit to build toward.

I destroy and break cycles of debt and cancel the spirit of bankruptcy in Jesus' name.

I decree and declare that I am a good steward over my finances.

I destroy and break every generational curse on both sides of my family, who were not faithful over what You had blessed them with.

I decree and declare that my head is anointed with God's oil and my cup runs over; goodness and mercy follow me all the days of my life (see Ps. 23:5).

I destroy and break verbal commitments or obligations that were presented falsely, in Jesus' name.

Day 57

Psalm 147:3

*He heals the brokenhearted and
bandages their wounds.*

God Heals Hurting Hearts

What a night you must had last night, My child. I have been
waiting to talk with you this morning. My child, I will heal your
wounds and bruises. Sometimes, we latch on to painful memo-
ries, disappointments, loneliness, or unforgiveness and will not
let them go. I am here to encourage you to keep going. Today is
your day for healing and restoration. I am re-engineering your inner man to clearly hear My voice. Allow the Holy Spirit's power
and presence to take control. Trust Me to heal your wounds. I am
purging wounding words from your ears and offenses from your
heart and replacing them with faith, encouragement, and hope.

Hurting people hurt other people. I will heal your relationships—from family ties to long-time friendships to business partnerships. Just like a revolving door, people will come in and out
of your life. Remain true to who you are in Christ. Love others
and look past their weaknesses. When you have the choice, choose
grace over condemnation. Remember if you judge someone, the
same judgment falls on you. Revisiting your past is not an option.
The enemy wants you to rehearse old hurts and offenses. Let us
live in the here and now; prepare yourself for what the future has
in store for you.

Scriptures

JOB 33:14, 5:18; JEREMIAH 30:17;
HOSEA 6:1; 1 CORINTHIANS 7:15

Breakthrough Prayer

I don't want to have false hopes or expectations about my friends and family. I am tired of being betrayed and let down by those I trusted. Father, relieve the stress and heal my broken heart. Your dunamis power can heal any person, situation, disease, problem, or trauma. Help me to rest in Your peace and remain hope-filled despite circumstances that try to drain and depleted my time, energy, and financial resources. In Jesus' name, I pray. Amen.

BREAKING CURSES AND RELEASING BLESSINGS
Day 57

I decree and declare that ill-spoken words will have no impact on my emotions in Jesus' name.

I destroy, overrule, and break ill-spoken words, ill wishes, enchantments, and every idle word spoken contrary to God's original plans and purposes.

I decree and declare that I am emotionally and mentally stable.

I destroy and break the spirit of revenge or ill thoughts and attempts of violence through anger, in Jesus' name.

I decree and declare I will represent and show the love of Christ.

I destroy and break myself free from false expectations and burdensome obligations in Jesus' name.

I decree and declare that I have favor with God and with man.

I destroy and break the invisible work of the enemy and release the fire of God to expose it now in Jesus' name.

I decree and declare that I am the head and not the tail, first and not last, above and not beneath, a lender and not a borrower, blessed and not cursed.

I destroy and break past wounds that try to open up through a memory or thought, in Jesus' name.

Day 58

Psalm 147:11

No, the Lord's delight is in those who fear him,
those who put their hope in his unfailing love.

God Delights in You

My child, Your concerns are My concerns. I am open to hear what is on your heart. Do not try to handle things alone. Believe that I will never fail you. I delight in those who obey Me and My precepts. Like David and his mighty army, I will empower you for battle and enable you to confront your enemies. David viewed accusations from a towering giant as an offense to Me. Instead of cowering in fear, holy boldness rose up inside of him and he confronted and killed Goliath. Follow David's example.

When people try to intimidate you and circumvent your God-given destiny, fight against evil. Whether a shepherd or soldier, David refused to doubt My provision and protection. You too must confront the giant of fear that wants to rattle you. Look to Me. Get in position. Stand your ground. Take your best shot. Watch as the giant in your life falls. Just as I supplied David with the arsenal to confront and defeat his enemy, I will do it for you.

Scriptures
1 Samuel 17; Romans 1:17;
Galatians 3:11; Hebrews 10:38

Breakthrough Prayer

I see that You delight in me when I fear You and rely on Your wisdom and counsel. When I feel afraid and struggle with a decision, You ask me to place my problems in Your loving hands and refuse to take them back. When I second-guess myself, Your love shatters all doubt that I am loved by You. In Jesus' name, I pray. Amen.

BREAKING CURSES AND RELEASING BLESSINGS
Day 58

I decree and declare that I am blessed in coming in and blessed going out.

I destroy and break off of myself greed and gluttony in Jesus' name.

I decree and declare that my decrees are established and legislative.

I destroy and break the spirit of disorder and any uncontrolled attitude from those who are in my company in Jesus' name.

I decree and declare that I am sober minded and make wise decisions for myself and others I love.

I destroy and break the counsel of the ignorant in Jesus' name.

I decree and declare no evil befalls me and no plague comes near my dwelling (see Ps. 91:10).

I destroy and break tactics of the enemy that rob me of my inheritance in the kingdom, in Jesus' name.

I decree and declare that I am rooted and grounded in love (see Eph. 3:17).

I destroy and break myself free any unwarranted attacks and problems sent by the devil, in Jesus' name.

Day 59

Proverbs 1:33

But all who listen to me will live in peace, untroubled by fear of harm.

God Wants You to Live in Peace

Change is coming! You are safe, My child. Pay attention to Me and relax. When chaos and confusion flood your mind, rest your head on My bosom. For fear opens the window for the adversary's schemes to enter in. I have sent the Holy Spirit to assist you in decision-making, relationships, business ventures, school, family, and ministry.

Faith is the opposite of fear. The whirlwind of life will want to instill fear in your heart. Walk in the earth like Enoch. He had a faith that caused him not to taste death but transition into My presence. Come against the noise of life that tries to distract your mind and close your ears to what I am saying. Listen for My still small voice. Obey My gentle whispers and walk with Me blameless and upright as Enoch did.

Scriptures
JOHN 3:8; EZEKIEL 37:9; HEBREWS 11:5;
ISAIAH 41:10; PROVERBS 2:6

Breakthrough Prayer

I am attentive to Your voice, Father. As I listen to You, I will not walk in fear or confusion. Help me tune out voices that try to compete with Yours. Break the "demonic chatter" that attempts to lead me astray. Let my ears reject earthly wisdom or carnal counsel. Teach me to discern what the Spirit is saying in this hour. In Jesus' name, I pray. Amen.

BREAKING CURSES AND RELEASING BLESSINGS
Day 59

I decree and declare that I have peace with God and the peace of God in my life.

I destroy and break the spirit of confusion and busyness in Jesus' name.

I decree and declare that I walk in the light as He is the Light and the blood of Jesus cleanses me daily from all sin (see 1 John. 1:7).

I destroy and break negative strongholds that come at times when I am weak or vulnerable.

I decree and declare that my children or spiritual children, mentees, and successors are taught of the Lord and great is their peace (see Isa. 54:13).

I destroy and break every pull that comes from seducing spirits to destroy my life, ministry, church, marriage, and relationships, in Jesus' name.

I decree and declare I am strengthened with might by God's Spirit in my inner man (see Eph. 3:16).

I destroy and break a losing mentality or attitude in Jesus' name.

I decree and declare that I am an overachiever and overcomer in Christ Jesus.

I destroy and break seasons of drought and desolation in Jesus' name.

Day 60

Proverbs 2:21

*For only the godly will live in the land, and
those with integrity will remain in it.*

God Will Give You the Land

Maintain your good name, My royal one. For a good name is better than riches. Enlarge your territory and influence what you put your hands to do. When you are working, stay focused. The spirit of distraction will try to derail you, but the Holy Spirit will get you back on track. You are on a winning team. You may feel like a rookie, but I have surrounded you with veterans who will train, equip, and prepare you to fulfill your destiny.

Your life is so valuable—worth more than gold and gemstones. Get with people who are grounded in the Word and who stay rooted in Me despite life's storms. I have settled your land. Continue walking in obedience and upright before Me. I promised Canaan to My covenant people and I kept that promise. Know My covenant extends to you.

Scriptures
Joshua 1:3; Deuteronomy 11:24;
Psalm 92:13-15, 84:11; Leviticus 20:24

Breakthrough Prayer

Father, I do not want to fall into deception and walk past a door or bypass an opportunity You ordained for me. Let the righteous dwell in the territory, region, and city that You have reserved as part of your kingdom plan. Give me the power to overcome trials and tribulations. In Jesus' name. Amen.

BREAKING CURSES AND RELEASING BLESSINGS
Day 60

I decree and declare that the Joshua anointing is upon me to gain and regain territory that is mine.

I destroy and break the spirit of fear, tiredness, and procrastination in Jesus' name.

I decree and declare that I walk in boldness and communicate the oracles of God to bring about change.

I destroy and break every enemy that is occupying that which is mine.

I decree and declare that I will live and enjoy the fruit of my labor in Jesus' name

I destroy, break, and bind every strong man in my city, region, territory, and home.

I decree and declare that I am alive in God through Christ (see Rom. 6:23).

I destroy and break all demonic influences and powers that will not comply with my commands, in Jesus' name.

I decree and declare that I am a possessor of Heaven and earth through Christ.

I destroy and break every spirit that comes to spy and send back reports of my success, in Jesus' name.

Day 61

PROVERBS 3:5-6

*Trust in the Lord with all your heart; do
not depend on your own understanding.
Seek his will in all you do, and he will
show you which path to take.*

God Directs Your Destiny

It is good to see you this morning. I rejoice when you pour out
your heart to Us. Trust that We have the solution to your problem.
I have been waiting to hear from you and for you to consult Me on
your next big move. Be a risk-taker. Take a leap of faith and do the
impossible. As you seek My will, rely on My supernatural knowledge and wisdom. I will impart revelation that will give an edge
that no one else has. When you rely on your own understanding,
you will soon realize you have limited access to the information you
need. If you depend on Me and My infinite "database," you will
never be disappointed.

When you are sold out to Me, some people may think you're a
fanatic. Do you know what nourished Jesus more than a meal? It
was doing His Father's will. That is what I require from you each
day to fulfill your prophetic destiny. It was Jesus' passion and desire
to align Himself with the mission I sent Him to the earth to accomplish. Do not be swayed by people's opinions or what you see.
Rely only on what you know by faith in My Word. Something is
stirring. Awaken the Holy Spirit's power and allow it to bubble
up inside of you. You can accomplish whatever you can envision.
When the enemy knocks the wind out of you, shake off a spirit
of condemnation or self-martyrdom. Let My love and redeeming
power undergird you.

Scriptures

JOHN 4:34, 6:38, 12:43; EPHESIANS 1:17;
ROMANS 8:1; TITUS 2:14; 1 CORINTHIANS 14:12

Breakthrough Prayer

I will trust in You with my very being—all of my heart, mind, and soul. My abilities, talents, and intellect can only take me so far. I will not be presumptuous. In all of my decisions, I will inquire and acknowledge You, Father. Thank You for sending the Holy Spirit to "speak" to my mind. In Jesus' name, I pray. Amen.

BREAKING CURSES AND RELEASING BLESSINGS

Day 61

I decree and declare that my destiny in God will not be altered and delayed.

I destroy and break the enemy of my destiny and purpose of the Lord in my life in Jesus' name.

I decree and release a kingdom anointing that will warrant favor and honor.

I destroy and break the power of dream killers and release the dream fulfillers in my life now in Jesus' name.

I decree and declare that I am in a king, and I break down high places of the enemy by the blood of Jesus (see Lev. 26:30).

I destroy and break every rooted sin and stubborn spirit that refuses to submit the lordship of Jesus Christ in my life.

I decree and declare that the high places in my life will become valleys and valley places become mountains of success for me.

Day 62

Psalm 42:5, NASB

Why are you in despair, O my soul? And why have you become disturbed within me? Hope in God, for I shall again praise Him for the help of His presence.

God Restores Your Hope

When your heart has been torn apart and your emotions are scattered like puzzle pieces, know that I not only will locate them but revive, restore, and return them their rightful place. I do not have to ask questions about what to do in your situation. I am the Answer! I am your Problem Solver! I am your Friend! I am here to place My arms around you when you need comfort. Let Me soothe the deepest wounds and hurts of your soul.

Within you, only I heal any aches and pains through the Holy Spirit's power. Are you willing to share those needs that have not been resolved yet? I am here for you to settle them for the last time. There is total hope and assurance in Me, My child. Allow Me to heal, restore, and mend those scars that we oftentimes refuse to look at. Some scars are not pleasant to look at, but they are your battle wounds and they are a testament of your bravery. Your tears speak volumes to Me even when you are silent. I hurt when you hurt. I want to let you know, My child, that I do understand and I will support you every step of the way.

Scriptures

Hosea 6:2; Psalm 30:11, 138:7; Jeremiah 31; Revelation 21:4; John 15:15; Hebrews 4:15

Breakthrough Prayer

I know that the weapons of my warfare are not carnal but mighty through You, Father. Train me to pull down every stronghold that comes to block me from seeing the Truth and walking in it. I will praise You with my lips. I am grateful that You come to my defense. In Jesus' name. Amen.

BREAKING CURSES AND RELEASING BLESSINGS
Day 62

I decree and declare that I am in a season of restoration and it will not be reversed.

I destroy and break the spirit of self-pity and the vagabond spirit in Jesus' name.

I decree and declare that I will walk in the hope of the glory of the Lord over my life.

I destroy and break any sabotage spirit against my calling and destiny that will bring expiration and termination.

I decree and declare that I shall tread upon the high places of the wicked in Jesus' name (see Deut. 33:29).

I destroy and break every false desire and passion that is not in agreement with the Word of God for my life.

I decree and declare that the high places our spiritual fathers destroyed will not be rebuilt, in Jesus' name (see 2 Chron. 33:3).

I destroy and break every enemy that comes in like a flood to overwhelm and overtake me.

I decree and declare that I will not lose sight of my God-given vision, objective, calling, and purpose.

I destroy and break every fraudulent relationship and spirit in Jesus' name.

Day 63

Psalm 43:5

*Why am I discouraged? Why is my heart so
sad? I will put my hope in God! I will praise
him again—my Savior and my God!*

God Brings Breakthrough for You

Do not give up, My friend and warrior. You have too much to
live for. Life revolves around Me and not the other way around. I
come to bring clarity and razor sharp discernment to distinguish
what season you are in. Do not get discouraged or bent out of
shape when your plans begin to unravel. I will tie the loose ends
together and weave them into a masterpiece. You are not in your
winter season, but you are coming into your spring season and a
new time of blessing. I come to let you know, My child, that you
are in your leap year, leap season, and leap of success.

Are you ready to leap over trials, tribulation, and adversity? Together we will break through the walls of resistance. I am listening
to every move you take in Me. My ears are ready to hear your
praises as you shout to Me. I will move Heaven and earth for you.
Even when you feel like a fighter cornered in the boxing ring, just
come out swinging and be determined to give your opponent a
mighty blow. It will be a flawless victory from a knockout punch
your enemy never expected. Resist the enemy so he will have no
other choice but to flee. I will protect you no matter what when
you call upon My name.

Scriptures
Psalm 17:6; 116:2; 121:7;
Haggai 2:6; James 4:7

Breakthrough Prayer

Thank You, Father, for leading me with Your love. I want to move in love and to allow Your love to engulf my heart. Show me the direction to take so that it does not lead me to a dead end. When I am sad, You know how to build me up again. I love You, Father. In Your name I pray. Amen.

BREAKING CURSES AND RELEASING BLESSINGS
Day 63

I decree and declare that the Lord of the breaker will enter into every facet and phase of my life for perpetual breakthroughs.

I destroy and break every opposing and hindering spirit sent for my demise, in Jesus' name.

I decree and declare that that righteous men and women with Your wisdom sit in the seat of governmental places of my city, region, state, and territory in Jesus' name (see Prov. 9:3).

I destroy and break demonic government, system, organization, and occultism representatives sent to suppress the believer of Christ.

I decree and declare that I walk in the spirit and not in the flesh in my day-to-day activities.

I destroy, dismantle, and break every exalted place and system that has positioned itself as the only and true living God.

I decree and declare that I am seated in heavenly places with Christ Jesus.

I destroy and break false intercessions and prayers sent diabolically against my life, family, church, city, business, and marriage, in Jesus' name.

I decree and declare that I am healthy and strong spiritually and physically.

I destroy and break curses of failure in Jesus' name.

Day 64

Psalm 9:10

Those who know your name trust in you, for you,
O Lord, do not abandon those who search for you.

God Knows You by Name

Start your day with worship so that I can visit you personally. I hear those who cry out to Me with a sincere heart and a contrite spirit. I know what you need and when you need it. I am eager for you to acknowledge Me. I am faithful and just to those who walk in My ways, statutes, and ordinances in My Word. My child, do not focus on what happened in the past or even on trials and hardships that threaten to alter your God-given path. Find your stability in Me; I will help you navigate through seasons of delay and accelerate your growth.

I will deliver you, My dear one, as I did the children of Israel. You have been adopted into My royal family. You are My child and I am pleased with you. I am delighted you have aligned yourself with Me and My kingdom. Trust in Me as your Sovereign Lord and your Provider. I am not slack in fulfilling My precious promises concerning you.

Scriptures
LUKE 10:27; DEUTERONOMY 6:5;
PROVERBS 3:6; 2 PETER 3:9; PSALM 54:4

Breakthrough Prayer

Father, I am grateful that You know every facet of my life. You know me by name. You know which direction I will soon take. Do not let me miss one moment. Break every limitation that comes into my life that could delay or detour my progress. In Jesus' name. Amen.

BREAKING CURSES AND RELEASING BLESSINGS
Day 64

I decree and declare that my name will not be removed from the Lamb's book of life.

I destroy and break every influence sent to take my attention off of Jesus Christ.

I decree and declare that I am loaded with spiritual gifts and they are being activated now in Jesus' name.

I destroy and break every negative thought and perception of me as a child of God.

I decree and declare that I will walk in the spirit and the liberty of the spirit.

I destroy and break the power of any sacrifice made in the high places with the blood of Jesus (see 1 Kings 3:2).

I decree and declare I will not be shaken, moved, altered, and shifted from my position and faith in Christ.

I destroy and break all negative stigma that come to defame, discredit, and place shame upon my name, in Jesus' name.

Day 65

Psalm 9:18

But the needy will not be ignored forever; the hopes of the poor will not always be crushed.

God Will Never Ignore You

Good morning, My child! I am conditioning you for what lies ahead. Understand, My child, that I will use you as an iron sharpener that will always stay relevant and on the cutting edge of what I am doing in your life. I will not allow you to be dull in this season. My desire is for you to be on the cutting edge of what I am doing. As you depend on Me, I will cause you to live out your God-driven dreams.

You have what it takes to blossom like a beautiful flower. Many will behold the greatness in you as you continue to put your faith and trust in Me. Know that I have given you keys that will open the doors to access, influence, and success. Are you ready to seize the day? Yield to My will as Esther did and begin to walk in your true identity. Fruitfulness first takes root in the heart. In everything you do, My desire is for you to produce fruit that is lasting and life changing. Your fruitfulness will not go unnoticed.

Scriptures
MATTHEW 16:19; PROVERBS 18:15-24, 27:17; COLOSSIANS 2:8

Breakthrough Prayer

I have tried to change myself, but realize that it is impossible without Your help. When I cry out to You, I know that You always hear me. Give me new ideas, concepts, and witty inventions that You have for me. In Jesus' name. Amen.

BREAKING CURSES AND RELEASING BLESSINGS
Day 65

I decree and declare that I am sharper and keener today than I was yesterday.

I destroy and break every soul tie that is not a pure covenant one established by God, in Jesus' name.

I decree and declare that God will honor and satisfy me with long life.

I destroy and break ungodly connections, relationships, and networks that produce corruption.

I decree and declare that my five senses are sharp and functional.

I destroy and break every demonic manipulation against my five senses, in Jesus' name.

I decree and declare that I get a favorable judgment and verdict.

I destroy and break all powers of mind control in Jesus' name.

I decree and declare that I am in my right mind and my name holds weight in the spirit.

I destroy and break myself free from relationships that have no godly credibility in Jesus' name.

Day 66

Psalm 10:17

*Lord, you know the hopes of the helpless. Surely
you will hear their cries and comfort them.*

God Helps the Helpless

Stay in My glorious presence. For haven't I commanded you in My Word to stop all activity and look to Me for help? When you meditate on My goodness and faithfulness, I will overshadow you with My lovingkindness. As you inhale and breathe deeply of My love, feel yesterday's cares and concerns lifting off your shoulders. Get ready for a shift in the atmosphere. See even now how the winds of change are starting to blow in your direction. Are you willing to flow in the gifts of My Spirit? The Holy Spirit comes to revive, restore, and reconstruct your most holy faith.

Just as a loving mother comforts her baby, I will hold you in My arms and reassure you that all is well. Remember, I have not given you the spirit of fear. Don't surrender to what life brings your way; instead, wave the white flag of worship unto Me. Jesus is the Way, the Truth, and the Life. My warrior child, know that I am going before you in battle to cause your enemies to succumb to their injuries. Every warrior goes into battle with weapons that are powerful, dependable, and capable of delivering a defeating blow to any adversary. Yield to Me and let Me wield you as a battle axe to crush your enemies.

Scriptures
Psalm 16:11, 46:10; Exodus 33:14; Isaiah 66:13;
2 Timothy 1:7; Matthew 11:28-30

Breakthrough Prayer

Holy Spirit, comfort me when I feel restless. Give me the courage and strength to overcome and endure. When I am in need of an answer, I know You will come to my rescue and give me the solution to life's problems and puzzles. Show me the truth of Your Word and reveal Yourself to me today. In Jesus' name. Amen.

BREAKING CURSES AND RELEASING BLESSINGS
Day 66

I decree and declare that I have angelic assistance and protection sent by Heaven on my behalf.

I destroy and break every temporary place that tries to become a permanent place in my life, in Jesus' name.

I decree and declare that more mercy is given daily as I am merciful to those in need and who have acted unjustly toward me.

I destroy and break old patterns and cycles that amount to no fruit.

I destroy and break idle or ignorant words or conversations spoken out of my mouth against leadership, my family, church, ministry, friends, and those in authority, in Jesus' name.

I decree and declare my destiny is navigated by the leading of the Holy Spirit and all detours are broken.

I destroy and break ungodly and diabolical movements that are not God in my life, in Jesus' name.

I decree and declare that I am in the right time and season of my life to advance the kingdom.

I destroy, bind, and break the spirit of mammon and a materialistic mentality for possession, money, and things, in Jesus' name.

Day 67

Psalm 12:5

The Lord replies, "I have seen violence done to the helpless, and I have heard the groans of the poor. Now I will rise up to rescue them, as they have longed for me to do."

God Will Be Your Bodyguard

Shout with a voice of triumph this morning. When you lift Me up high, watch how people's hearts are open and ready to receive what I have for them. The Lion of the tribe of Judah goes before you. Today make it your business to declare that fear and deception will have no hold on you, My child. Be alert so you do not fall victim to the enemy's deceptive tactics. Counter the enemy's roar by releasing a ferocious sound of your own.

My child, I have intercepted the darts that the enemy sent to break your rhythm. I am watching over you and will not allow you to be helpless. I have heard your petitions to meet your needs and those of your loved ones. I'm coming to help you navigate your troubles, redeem your days, and return you to your true identify and authority in Jesus. Believe with your whole heart that what was lost will be returned to you.

Scriptures
Psalm 47:1, 121:5-8; Revelation 5:5;
2 Chronicles 20:22; Acts 17:11

Breakthrough Prayer

Father, protect me from being deceived and falling victim to the roaming and roaring lion. Strengthen my resolve and renew my hope. As my heart is open before You, show me how to speak words of faith and victory over every circumstance I face. In Jesus' name. Amen.

BREAKING CURSES AND RELEASING BLESSINGS

Day 67

I ask and declare that God will release Archangel Michael to war on my behalf.

I destroy and break the spiritual powers of the roaring lion and ravenous bear to bring death and destruction, in Jesus' name.

I decree and declare that I walk in the path of the righteous.

I destroy and break into pieces the bars of iron and gates of brass that deny me access.

I decree and declare that I have the grace to fulfill every detail of my calling and assignment in the earth.

I destroy and break into pieces every evil mountain in my path and command them to hear the voice of the Lord to never resurrect.

I decree and declare I am a joint heir with Christ (see Rom. 8:17).

I destroy and break every illegal and demonic bond and link in the spirit in Jesus' name.

I decree and declare that my body is a member of the Body of Christ and I am aligned properly (see 1 Cor. 6:15).

I destroy and break every demonic declaration, proclamation, and decree that is sent as an assault against my life, in Jesus' name.

Day 68

Psalm 13:5-6

*But I trust in your unfailing love. I will
rejoice because you have rescued me. I will
sing to the Lord because he is good to me.*

God's Love Is Endless and Unfailing

Sing a new song, My child. Let Me hear a new melody straight from your heart to Mine. This love song brings joy and pleasure to My heart. I will be good to those who know Me as their Deliverer and Savior. My redemptive power has caused you to shift into a new realm of possibility and favor. You are a shining star that displays My glory and marvelous light to a hurting world.

My child, I will never give up on you because Jesus paid a dear price to redeem you. I love you with a love that is everlasting and faithful. Be yourself no matter what others say or think. Never change who you are to fit in or win people's approval. My child, I fashioned you for greatness—you possess unique spiritual gifts, natural talents, and a distinct personality like no other. Only you can discover your potential and release it into a world that has been waiting to receive all you have to offer.

Scriptures
ZEPHANIAH 3:17; JEREMIAH 32:41;
GALATIANS 3:13; ACTS 17:11

Breakthrough Prayer

I thank You for Your unfailing love toward me. You have not given up on me when others have. Holy Spirit, reveal those broken places and use Your redemptive power to bring healing. I want to be pleasing in Your sight, Father. In Jesus' name. Amen.

BREAKING CURSES AND RELEASING BLESSINGS
Day 68

I decree and declare that I am highly favored of the Lord.

I destroy and break the enemy of my soul and cover myself with the blood of the Lamb in Jesus' name.

I decree and declare that I am unstoppable, unmovable, and unbothered by satan's strategies.

I destroy and break demonic markers of identification.

I decree and declare that I take spiritual audits of my spiritual progress and growth and they are not stifled.

I destroy and break slander and self-incrimination against my life, name, work, and character.

I decree and declare that I am triumphant in Christ (see 1 Cor. 15:57).

I destroy and break the landscape of quicksand set up by the enemy to cause me to sink and die.

I decree and declare that I am in the right place at the right time doing the right thing with the right anointing.

I destroy and break the spirit of robbery that comes to seize the favor of God on my life, in Jesus' name.

Day 69

Psalm 16:8

*I know the Lord is always with me. I will
not be shaken, for he is right beside me.*

God Is Your Constant Companion

You framed your world with your words. After all, life and
death are in the power of the tongue. Change your words and
you change your circumstance. You have the authority to change
circumstances with one word. You are a world changer. I will cause
you to activate your faith and to wait and watch as things begin to
change for the better. I am never far from you; I am always right
by your side. The Holy Spirit lives inside of you and directs every
step you take.

Take a few minutes today to write down the vision I have placed
in your heart. Declare it out loud with boldness, clarity, and confidence. Understand that as you put pen to paper your vision is
activated. I will cause My angels to hear your declaration and go
ahead of you to gather the resources needed to construct and complete your vision. As a seed planted in fertile soil, I have deposited
a vision in your spirit, which I will nurture and cultivate until it is
completed in your lifetime. Over time you will see the harvest of
blessings that will be the fruit others will be blessed by.

Scriptures
HEBREWS 11:3; DEUTERONOMY 31:8; HABAKKUK 2:2-3

Breakthrough Prayer

Jesus, clear my vision that I may see the way You see things. Give me the pen of Heaven that I may write Your vision on my heart. Thank You, Father, for standing alongside me in tough times. I need that extra support from sunrise to sunset. In Jesus' name. Amen.

BREAKING CURSES AND RELEASING BLESSINGS

Day 69

I decree and declare that I am in right standing with the Lord.

I destroy and break myself free from unhealthy and worldly relationships in Jesus' name.

I decree and declare that I am sanctified in Christ Jesus (see 1 Cor. 1:2).

I destroy and break the spirit of unproductivity in Jesus' name.

I decree and declare that I have been chosen before the foundation of the world that I should be holy and without blame before Him (see Eph. 1:4).

I destroy and break all powers of hell that come to destabilize me from advancing the King and His kingdom,

I decree and declare that I have liberty in Christ (see Gal. 2:4).

I destroy and break all chains of resistance that try to keep me from serving God with all of my heart, mind, and strength, in Jesus' name.

I decree and declare that I am crucified with Christ (see Gal. 2:20).

I destroy and break sudden sickness, illness, common colds, restlessness, and fatigue that comes to stop me, in Jesus' name.

Day 70

Psalm 18:1-6

I love you, Lord; you are my strength. The Lord is my rock, my fortress, and my savior; my God is my rock, in whom I find protection. He is my shield, the power that saves me, and my place of safety. I called on the Lord, who is worthy of praise, and he saved me from my enemies. The ropes of death entangled me; floods of destruction swept over me. The grave wrapped its ropes around me; death laid a trap in my path. But in my distress I cried out to the Lord; yes, I prayed to my God for help. He heard me from his sanctuary; my cry to him reached his ears.

God Will Save You from the Evil One

Together, we can construct your life. Let us build a life that has more than you could ever imagine or dream. Where can you find grace when you need it? It is impossible to earn My grace. Do not bypass My power and venture out on your own to change your circumstances. Pray for the change you want to see. I will save you time and time again with My life-giving power.

Watch as I open wide the windows of Heaven and flood your soul with My sustaining grace. No longer will oppression, stress, fear, unbelief, doubt, and anxiety overshadow you. Your prayers and petitions have reached Me. Know that I am merciful, but I am also holy and just. Nothing escapes My watchful eyes.

Scriptures
Haggai 2:9; Psalm 16:8, 18:2; Isaiah 54:10;
1 Corinthians 15:58; Exodus 1:12

Breakthrough Prayer

Jesus, I want to experience Your glory in my life. I am renewed and strengthened as I commune with You. My faith has been tested. My character has been tried. Through it all, You have caused me to prevail through my travail. In Jesus' name. Amen.

BREAKING CURSES AND RELEASING BLESSINGS

Day 70

I decree and declare that the Lord is the Rock of my salvation.

I destroy and disallow any illegal attacks from the north, south, west, and east in Jesus' name.

I decree and declare that I have victory through Jesus (see 1 Cor. 15:57).

I destroy and disallow any demonic intelligence, opinion, teaching, doctrine, and literature in my sphere of activity in Jesus' name.

I decree and declare that I have been quickened with Christ (see Eph. 2:6).

I destroy and break every spiritual bacteria that comes to invade my life, in Jesus' name.

I decree and declare I am complete in Christ and my life is hid with Him in God (see Col. 2:10; 3:3).

I destroy and break premature death and premature birthing to the God-given dream in my heart.

I decree and declare that Christ is my life and the central focus of all that I do in the earth (see Col. 3:4).

I destroy and break obstacles of the enemy that are an offense to the purposes of God in my life, in Jesus' name.

Day 71

Psalm 20:6-8

Now I know that the Lord rescues his anointed king. He will answer him from his holy heaven and rescue him by his great power. Some nations boast of their chariots and horses, but we boast in the name of the Lord our God. Those nations will fall down and collapse, but we will rise up and stand firm.

God Will Help You Pass Life's Tests

Tests and trials come to reveal your true mettle. You have been made to conquer and subdue your enemies. Not only I have given you authority, but you are My image-bearer. You are made in My image according to My likeness. You were born with My DNA! The very fact that you were created causes the universe to greatly admire My masterpiece. Today, I am releasing blessings beyond measure over your life. I will continue providing all that you need simply because you asked and acknowledge Me by walking in obedience to My Word and My commands.

I am looking for those who will put their confidence in Me and not their bank account, careers, or properties. The earth is Mine and the fullness therein. I own everything, so why not believe in My faithfulness and love? Your desire is My desire. You never have to beg for what belongs to a child of the King. Today, declare that unexpected blessings are headed your way.

Scriptures

Psalm 20:7, 24:7; 1 Corinthians 10:26; Deuteronomy 10:14; 1 John 4:4; James 1:18

Breakthrough Prayer

Heavenly Father, You passed along Your spiritual DNA to me and made me in Your image and likeness. I have been given dominion over the powers of the enemy. You have planted my feet and caused me to flourish. Give me more strategies that I will know how to navigate through life's path so that I will not be left behind. In Jesus' name. Amen.

BREAKING CURSES AND RELEASING BLESSINGS
Day 71

I decree and declare that I will pass every test and trial that life throws my way.

I destroy and break every channel and portal built to block my blessing, in Jesus' name.

I decree and declare that I have been created in Christ unto good work (see Eph. 2:6).

I destroy and break every circumstance, situation, problem, issue, and dilemma that comes to upset me, in Jesus' name.

I decree and declare that I have boldness and access in Christ (see Eph. 3:12).

I destroy and break every spirit that comes to bring stagnation and slothfulness in Jesus' name.

I decree and declare that every test or examination that I take, I will pass with a high score needed to qualify me.

I destroy and break the patterns of failure or disappointment that come as a result of not being qualified.

I decree and declare that I can do all things through Christ who strengthens me in every situation I find myself in (see Phil. 4:19).

I destroy and break any connections and relationships that would produce failure, lack, or pain, in Jesus' name.

Day 72

Psalm 22:3-5

*Yet you are holy, enthroned on the praises of Israel.
Our ancestors trusted in you, and you rescued
them. They cried out to you and were saved.
They trusted in you and were never disgraced.*

God Saves Those Who Call on Him

Release your faith today for the supernatural. Miracles, signs, and wonders are available to you. You will release light in dark places and be a voice to the voiceless. I do not play favorites. Rain falls on the just and the unjust. Know that you are favored of the Lord. Joseph's colorful coat attracted the good, the bad, and the ugly, but he was repeatedly protected from the enemy's plan to strip him of his identity, power, and calling. Follow his example and stand firm despite the pitfalls devised to unravel your belief in Me and My promises.

Never be content with your present condition. Challenge yourself to be better, do better, and live better. Know, My child, that there are many believers before you who have paved the way while paying a high price for what they have obtained. By faith they served their generation and walked in faithful obedience. You too are a trailblazer, scouting out the land and charting a path for others to follow your example. As you imitate Me, others will imitate you. Keep your motives pure and your heart humble. My child, in due season you will reap what you so generously sowed into the lives of other people.

Scriptures
Mark 16:17-18; John 1:5; Psalm 5:12, 119:9;
Genesis 37, 1:27; Proverbs 4:23

Breakthrough Prayer

Holy Spirit, You come to equip, counsel, and direct me. Through the eyes of faith, I see things clearly. Give me a heart like David to serve my generation, and when my time is done I will leave this earth with honor. In Jesus' name. Amen.

BREAKING CURSES AND RELEASING BLESSINGS

Day 72

I decree and declare that my salvation will not be taken for granted.

I destroy and break myself free from any company of wickedness and evil in Jesus' name.

I decree and declare that I have liberty, emancipation, and freedom in the Holy Spirit and in Christ (see Gal. 2:4).

I destroy and break pressures of life and expected worries that are not mine, in Jesus' name.

I decree and declare that I have safety in the presence of God and I will not be abandoned.

I destroy and break every agenda of the past that will try to resurface old issues and hurts in my new season.

I decree and declare I will rejoice in Christ and press toward the mark of the high calling of God in Christ (see Phil. 3:3,14).

I destroy and break all spirits of backbiting, gossip, retaliation, and anger from those who operate in jealousy, envy, or hatred for no reason against me.

I decree and declare that God will supply all of my needs through Christ Jesus (see Phil. 4:19).

I destroy and break every pit set up against me in Jesus' name.

Day 73

Psalm 22:24

For he has not ignored or belittled the suffering of the needy. He has not turned his back on them, but has listened to their cries for help.

God Will Never Turn Away from You

Set sail toward the next destination. I want you to resolve some issues in order for you to move on. Do not let stressful situations stir up any resentment, offense, or unforgiveness hidden in your heart. As these dark clouds pass by, know that I am causing the sun to break through for you.

Know that trials, tribulations, and tests come to build the character of Christ within you—not to crush you. The time is right for to take your ideas to the next level. You can do it; I believe in you. I will not leave you hanging or turn My back on you. We are in it to win it!

Scriptures
Proverbs 28:9; Deuteronomy 1:45;
Matthew 10:22; 1 Peter 4:12-19

Breakthrough Prayer

I have weathered the storm because of Your protection, Holy Spirit. Safeguard me from any unexpected storms and winds that blow. You are my umbrella that covers me from all harm. I am delighted that You cheer me on even when others are against me. In Jesus' name. Amen.

BREAKING CURSES AND RELEASING BLESSINGS

Day 73

I decree and declare that my life is functioning according to Heaven's timetable and calendar for my life.

I destroy and break every diabolical clock set up to alarm and work against me to frustrate my God season, in Jesus' name.

I decree and declare that I am a partaker of Christ and preserved in Christ (see Heb. 3:14; Jude 1:1).

I destroy and break illegal and ungodly strings of attachment that have been established out of ignorance in Jesus' name.

I decree and declare that I am dead with Christ and my life is not my own (see Col. 1:27).

I destroy and break any drought in my life caused by myself or those I came into covenant without God's direction.

I decree and declare that I have peace within in my walls and prosperity within my palace (see Ps. 122:7).

I destroy and break confusion, division, disorder, and quarreling within my walls and poverty within my gates.

I decree and declare that I am an ambassador of Christ and speak on the behalf of His kingdom.

I destroy and break any league and alliance of satan in my city, region, state, nation, and territory in Jesus' name.

Day 74

Psalm 23:1-4

The Lord is my shepherd; I have all that I need. He lets me rest in green meadows; he leads me beside peaceful streams. He renews my strength. He guides me along right paths, bringing honor to his name. Even when I walk through the darkest valley, I will not be afraid, for you are close beside me. Your rod and your staff protect and comfort me.

God Renews Your Strength

Be quick to hear My voice this day, My child. There are streams of wisdom, knowledge, and information that I want to share, but they are not for those with haughty hearts or puffed up spirits. For I resist the proud and extend grace to the humble. Stay in step with Me throughout the day. Do not lag behind or run out in front of Me. Take My hand and follow My lead. I know your beginning and your ending.

Believe that all of Heaven's resources are available to you. Let Me renew your strength when you are weary or weak. I will raise you up when people put you down. I am the Good Shepherd who wards off the wolves and demonic predators assigned to your name and calling.

Scriptures
Ephesians 1:17; Isaiah 40:28-31, 41:10

Breakthrough Prayer

When I am drained and I can't go any further, I am reminded that Your Word is alive and able to rejuvenate my soul. You are a Good Shepherd who feeds me when I am hungry and quenches my thirsty soul. In Jesus' name. Amen.

BREAKING CURSES AND RELEASING BLESSINGS
Day 74

I decree and declare that God is renewing my mind, body, and soul.

I destroy and break every leech and spirit that comes to drain me of my resources, strength, and anointing, in Jesus' name.

I decree and declare that I am no longer in my molting season like an eagle but I have renewed strength to mount up on wings to soar.

I destroy and bind the Leviathan spirit of pride and the python spirit of divination in my life, church, family, ministry, city, state, and region in Jesus' name.

I decree and declare that the arrows of deliverance, healing, and miracles will impact and touch nations.

I destroy and break numbness of the mind and incomprehension to the truth.

I decree and declare that I am prosperous in all that I am called to do and that God is sending me laborers to assist with my vision.

I destroy and break burnout, exhaustion, strain, and weakness that comes because of work.

I decree and declare that my vats overflow continually in my life, family, business, church, ministry, and divine relationships.

I destroy and break the arrows of the enemy sent to take me out suddenly in Jesus' name.

Day 75

Psalm 23:5

You prepare a feast for me in the presence of my enemies. You honor me by anointing my head with oil. My cup overflows with blessings.

God's Anointing Overflows in Your Life

Good morning, My child! Are you ready to enter into a place flowing with milk and honey? Are you ready to do the impossible for Me? If the answer is yes, then get ready for a wonderful ride in the Spirit. I am pouring fresh wine into new wineskins, preserving the best for last. Have I not declared in My Word what is last shall be first and what is first shall be last? My child, your enemies will eat the slanderous words spoken against you. I am causing your value and self-worth to increase.

You will begin to attract those who will serve instead of drain your energy, bless instead of curse you, pray for you instead of preying on you, and anoint instead of annoy you. Move beyond your comfort zone. That is where miracles happen. Learn from the widow of Zarephath's faith and Elijah's obedience. Get your buckets out and declare—supernatural provision will flow freely today from Heaven and all my needs will be met.

Scriptures
EXODUS 16, 33:3, 8; 1 KINGS 17; MATTHEW 9:17, 19:30; MARK 2:22; LUKE 20:43; PSALM 110:1; ACTS 2:35

Breakthrough Prayer

Humility comes before honor. You anoint my head with Your Holy Spirit. Anoint my head and empower me to do greater works. Father, crown me with honor as I obey Your Word and will. Raise my expectation for miracles as You move me outside my comfort zone. In Jesus' name. Amen.

BREAKING CURSES AND RELEASING BLESSINGS
Day 75

I decree and declare that the anointing oil on my life will not be stopped but continue to flow as I am in right position in God. *I destroy* every blockage of the oil that God has placed in my life in Jesus' name.

I decree and declare that the anointing of God on my life will not be prostituted, used for personal gain, and merchandized.

I destroy and break the Judas spirit that tries to come in my sphere of ministry, work, or career to mismanage the resources that God has entrusted me with in Jesus' name.

I decree and declare that the heavens are declaring the glory of God over my life (see Ps. 19:1).

I destroy and break every false leadership and influence that operates in deception, greed, and corruption in Jesus' name.

I decree and declare that my anointing is to be used for the glory of God only.

I destroy and break any compromises and negotiations that are not for the glory and purpose of the kingdom.

I decree and declare that my gaze will be set upon the Lord and that I have dove eyes to see into the sun (Son, Jesus Christ).

I destroy and break the spirit of fear of the supernatural and the gifts of the spirit in Jesus' name.

Day 76

Psalm 23:6

*Surely your goodness and unfailing love will
pursue me all the days of my life, and I will
live in the house of the Lord forever.*

God's Favor Follows You

Do you hear a knock on the door? I am standing outside, waiting for you to open the door. You've been steadfast and immoveable and now the wait is over. You have selflessly sacrificed your resources. It's graduation day. Time to move My beloved to the next level in the Spirit. Do not allow life to keep you complacent and stagnant. My dear child, Jesus is the Doorway into the supernatural realm of favor and anointing. Let Me surround you with My goodness, favor, and unfailing love all the days of your life.

As you continue on your spiritual journey, I will keep pouring My amazing grace on you every step of the way. You have been asking when, what, and how these provisions will come your way. Consider this: What you have been looking for is now looking for you. What you have been asking for is now asking for you. Favor will call you blessed! What is Ours is yours, and I will block anyone who feels they desire what I have placed upon you. Your faithfulness unto Me has not gone unnoticed. Goodness will chase you, favor will overtake you, and peace will massage you!

Scriptures
Matthew 7:7-8; Jeremiah 29:13; Luke 11:9;
Revelation 22:13; John 15:16

Breakthrough Prayer

I want to grow in You and become more like Jesus. I want to experience Your sacrificial love. Shower me with Your favor as You open up the heavens over my life. Rain down Your provision so I can meet the needs around me. In Your name. Amen.

BREAKING CURSES AND RELEASING BLESSINGS
Day 76

I decree and declare that the favor of God on my life will open opportunities that money cannot open for me.

I destroy and break jealousy from around me due to the favor of God on my life in Jesus' name.

I decree and declare that everything that my hands touch will multiply and have great success.

I destroy and break the powers of misfortune and lack in Jesus' name.

I decree and declare that I am a winner and finisher in Christ.

I destroy and break scandalous dealings within my sphere of influence and activity in Jesus' name.

I decree and declare that God has dealt wondrously with me; I shall eat and be satisfied (see Joel 2:26).

I destroy and break the spirit of contradiction that comes from those who are in authority.

I decree and declare that the plowman overtakes the reaper in my life, and the treader of grapes, the sower of the seed, and I live in continual harvest blessings in Jesus' name (see Amos 9:13).

I destroy and bind every crow, pigeon, black bird, or vulture that comes to eat up my seed and harvest, in Jesus' name.

Day 77

Psalm 25:10

*The Lord leads with unfailing love and faithfulness
all who keep his covenant and obey his demands.*

God's Love Is Covenantal

Love covers a multitude of faults; My love never fails. It was My love for this world that caused Me to sacrifice My only begotten Son. You were on My mind when I sent Jesus to redeem humanity. Many will see the power and authority of your God released through you. There will be those, My child, who will come to challenge your relationship with Me but are seducing you into an alternative way to break covenant. Be watchful of those who have hidden agendas because of what I am doing in you and through you.

You will know those who are sold out to Jesus and those who are not interested except in what the world offers. Your destiny is linked in Me. I am at work in your life. The innate gifts in you belong to you and you alone. The earth has need of what you have to offer. Never settle for less. I faithfully keep My covenant that I established with your ancestors. You will become a tree that will produce many branches that will bear much fruit. My love toward you becomes your lifeline and covenantal promise of success.

Scriptures
1 Peter 4:8, Proverbs 10:12; Ephesians 1:7;
Matthew 5:7; Deuteronomy 7:9

Breakthrough Prayer

Holy Spirit, You have been sent to help me in my Christian walk. I don't want to be found unfaithful. I thank You, Father, that in all that I have done Your love has covered me. My past sins have no more power over me. You are faithful in keeping Your promises as I obey Your Word and covenant. In Jesus' name. Amen.

BREAKING CURSES AND RELEASING BLESSINGS
Day 77

I decree and declare that I will walk in covenantal blessings of the Lord.

I destroy and break from around me any covenant breaches and breakers in Jesus' name.

I decree and declare that my floor is full of wheat and my vats overflow with wine and oil (see Joel 2:25).

I destroy and break all unusual and suspicious activities in my life, family, city, and region in Jesus' name.

I decree and declare that I will walk circumspect before the Lord.

I destroy and break every spiritual violator that comes with forced entry, in Jesus' name.

I decree and declare that I will walk with men and women of God who have integrity.

I destroy and break the spirit of immaturity that comes within my sphere of influence and work.

I decree and declare that the Lord had brought me into a land without scarceness or lack (see Deut. 8:9).

I destroy and break any tragedies that has been produced by the enemy of my destiny, in Jesus' name.

Day 78

Psalm 27:1-2

*The Lord is my light and my salvation—
so why should I be afraid? The Lord is my
fortress, protecting me from danger, so why
should I tremble? When evil people come
to devour me, when my enemies and foes
attack me, they will stumble and fall.*

God Is Your Salvation and Light

Balance is critical to making sound decisions. My child, you will no longer find yourself tottering on life's balancing beam. Let Me hide you in My secret place. No fiery darts, lies, or temptations. The accuser wants to short-circuit My power from flowing in you. He wants to intimidate you and deceive you into thinking he's a roaring lion that will devour your dreams. Know that what was meant for evil meant for your destruction, I'm turning it around for your construction.

I will shine My everlasting light in every area of your life. I will continually keep you out of harm's way. You do not ever have to worry about losing control because I am your peace in the midst of any storm. Know that you also do not have to be concerned about things that are not relevant to your divine breakthrough. I have come to break and shake everything that can be shaken and broken in your life for you to receive your blessing. I will turn the tables of your enemies and they will become your waiter and host of blessing. Rest in My presence and be secure in your salvation that is locked and linked in My dear Son, Jesus!

Scriptures
PROVERBS 2:6, 28:15; 2 CORINTHIANS 6:14;
PHILIPPIANS 4:8; 1 PETER 5:8

Breakthrough Prayer

Jesus, keep me from danger seen and unseen. Protect me from the enemy's arrows and relentless attacks designed to destroy me. I will not self-destruct or back down; instead, I decree and declare today that I have victory. In Your name. Amen.

BREAKING CURSES AND RELEASING BLESSINGS
Day 78

I decree and declare that the light of the kingdom of God shines brighter in my life.

I destroy and break the work of darkness that comes to bring fear and blindness.

I decree and declare that when I am weak, Christ is made strong in me.

I destroy and break the spirit of delusion or a reprobate mind of those who have moved in the realm of perversion and pride, in Jesus' name.

I decree and declare that the rocks pour out rivers of oil in my life, family, ministry, marriage, church, and business (see Job 29:6).

I destroy and break every demonic spirit that comes back in opportune times to cause me to fall into sin or backslide, in Jesus' name.

I decree and declare my life will be a living epistle read by men.

I destroy and break the systems of men that cause people to move in error or ignorance.

I decree and declare that my feet are planted and my steps are ordered by the Lord.

I destroy and bind all works of witchcraft against the work of Christ in my life through the Holy Spirit, in Jesus' name.

Day 79

Psalm 27:4-5

*The one thing I ask of the Lord—the thing I
seek most—is to live in the house of the Lord
all the days of my life, delighting in the Lord's
perfections and meditating in his Temple.
For he will conceal me there when troubles
come; he will hide me in his sanctuary. He
will place me out of reach on a high rock.*

God Is Your Sanctuary

Create a dwelling place for Me within your heart. My child, I
am not interested with simply visiting you. I am looking for a holy
habitation, a place where I can live, move, and have My very being
in you. There is no other place I long to be but with you day after
day. I want to reveal Myself to you in ways that you have never
known before. As I make My home in your heart, there's no longer
any room for anyone or anything other than Me.

The more we fellowship, the more our hearts are intertwined.
There is synchronicity in this secret place. As we spend quality
time together in the secret place, I cover you with My protecting
presence. Despite every destructive force and measure that comes
your way by the devil, stand on Christ the solid Rock. Face your
toughest critics, opponents, and detractors with the Word of God.
Worship will change your atmosphere causing the glory to come.

Scriptures
Jude 1:20; Psalm 91, 37:4; Job 1:10

Breakthrough Prayer

Father, ignite a fire and set me ablaze. Pour out fresh oil that will keep the fire burning. I want to be Your fire-starter. Keep me from the enemy who wants to extinguish the fire. In Jesus' name. Amen.

BREAKING CURSES AND RELEASING BLESSINGS
Day 79

I decree and declare that I have a prayer mountain and altar of worship in my heart before the Lord.

I destroy and break into pieces all satanic altars of Baal in Jesus' name.

I decree and declare that the angels of blessings will not depart from me without blessing me.

I destroy, dismantle, and break all demonic sanctuaries and portals in Jesus' name.

I decree and declare that I love wisdom, I will inherit substance, and my treasures are filled at all times.

I destroy and break every demonic invasion or infestation in my life, city, region, and territory in Jesus' name.

I decree and declare I shall inherit the land for the purpose and usage of the kingdom.

I destroy and burn satanic wombs that have been created through conception of demonic thoughts, ideas, and agendas.

I decree and declare that the Lord will bring me honey out of the rock (see Ps. 81:16).

I destroy and break into pieces every stumbling block or rock to trip me up from moving forward in life, in Jesus' name.

Day 80

Psalm 27:10-11

*Even if my father and mother abandon me,
the Lord will hold me close. Teach me how
to live, O Lord. Lead me along the right
path, for my enemies are waiting for me.*

God Will Not Forsake You

Search my heart, mind, and soul. As you diligently seek Me, My ear is tuned to your prayers and worship. Come and let My abiding presence wash over you and immerse yourself in lavish love. Never stop chasing after Me. Be a God-chaser for your generation. As you walk by faith and not by sight, you'll gain a greater awareness and sensitivity to My Spirit. People can reject, abandon, ridicule, and set you back, but I come to embrace, love, restore, and set you up to walk in total victory.

The enemy comes to break you in to submitting to life's rifts and cliffs. I come to break off of you the illegal attachment and agreements that the enemy thinks he has on you. I will never abandon what I have called Mine. In My presence, we become one and a unit that cannot be broken. I will teach you how to live in the Spirt and not walk in the fleshly appetites that the world tends to bring to your table. Eat of My Word and become that fresh manna that the world will listen to and feast upon. I am your Pathway and Pathfinder in a murky world.

Scriptures
JOHN 14:16, 23; 2 CORINTHIANS 5:7;
MARK 4:39; ROMANS 12:2

Breakthrough Prayer

When I feel abandoned by friends and family, I know You will never leave or forsake me. Continue teaching me how to receive Your amazing grace and listen to Your gentle whispers. Holy Spirit, help me stay on the narrow road that leads to righteousness. In Jesus' name. Amen.

BREAKING CURSES AND RELEASING BLESSINGS
Day 80

I decree and declare that I am a child, king-priest, and joint heir of Christ.

I destroy and break the patterns of rejection that come from those I love or those in authority.

I decree and declare that the blessings of God shall be upon my storehouses, banking accounts, and barrels.

I destroy and break the work of dysfunction, malfunction, and the spirit of insanity in Jesus' name.

I decree and declare that my barns are full and overflowing, my sheep bring forth thousands and ten thousands, my oxen are strong to labor (see Ps. 144:13-14).

I destroy, bind, and break every spirit that was unleashed from hell against my life, family, church, ministry, marriage, business, and city, in Jesus' name.

I decree and declare that I am a child of God and I am not forsaken by Him.

I destroy and break the orphan spirit and dependence on others to provide.

I decree and declare that all grace is being released toward me because I have all sufficiency in all things and abound to every good work (see 2 Cor. 9:8).

I destroy and break every bad habit that creates a bad cycle in my life, in Jesus' name.

Day 81

Psalm 28:7-8

The Lord is my strength and shield. I trust him with all my heart. He helps me, and my heart is filled with joy. I burst out in songs of thanksgiving. The Lord gives his people strength. He is a safe fortress for his anointed king.

God Is Your Song of Thanksgiving

When you hear the signal, run your race from start to finish. My child, the enemy wants to cause you to have false starts in your life. His intent is to disqualify you before your feet ever leave the starting blocks. Know that the Commander of the angel armies has interrupted his secret plan. I have exposed his plot against you. Declare with a shout today—enough is enough. I am positioning you to take back the ground relinquished to the accuser of the brethren. Pray your victory into existence.

Let us build up your faith muscles. For the race is not promised to the fastest or strongest runner, but to those who endure to the end. Watch and wait for Me this morning. I look forward to hearing you sing a song of thanksgiving from your heart. You know that I will inhabit your praises. Worship is a powerful weapon in your arsenal. Yield to the Holy Spirit and follow His marching orders. He will help you dodge the enemy's hits and defeat the enemy.

Scriptures
2 Timothy 4:7-8; 1 Corinthians 9:24-27;
Ecclesiastes 9:11; Psalm 147:7; Jeremiah 30:19

Breakthrough Prayer

Father, I will run my race well so I'm not disqualified. I don't want to stay stuck in my routine but accelerate full speed ahead in the Spirit. Surround me with people who love You and obey Your commandments. In Jesus' name. Amen.

BREAKING CURSES AND RELEASING BLESSINGS

Day 81

I decree and declare that my mouth will release the praise of Judah.

I destroy and break every battle at the edge of my breakthrough now in Jesus' name.

I decree and declare that there is a new song in my heart to sing daily to the Lord.

I destroy and break every curse against my salvation and relationship with the Lord Jesus.

I decree and declare that I will sing songs of salvation that will bring joy to someone's life daily.

I destroy and release the fire of God onto every wicked and perverted power now that is sitting on my breakthrough, in Jesus' name.

I decree and declare that every evil eye looking, monitoring, and influencing my destiny be blinded and destroyed now in Jesus' name.

I destroy and break hardness of heart toward the truth of God's Word in the Body of Christ.

I decree and declare that many souls will come unto the Lord in my generation.

I destroy and break every wall of perdition and division in regions where the gospel of Jesus is hard to penetrate, in Jesus' name.

Day 82

Psalm 28:9

*Save your people! Bless Israel, your special
possession. Lead them like a shepherd,
and carry them in your arms forever.*

God Blesses His People

Good morning, My child. When I look at you, I see My love
bestowed upon you each and every day. This love creates a musical
harmony declaring My love for you and your love for Me. Run
into My loving arms. Like a good Father, I will not allow you to
settle in one place too long or get comfortable in a routine for
very long. It is time to shake off the dust. Life is filled with painful
bumps, bruises, and scars as you experience growing pains. When
you fall, brush yourself off and keep moving forward.

I come with life-giving power. I can deliver you from the traps,
trials, or temptations. My child, let wisdom, self-control, and discernment stop your cravings from carrying you away. The enemy's
strategy is to undermine our relationship. Be persistent, resilient,
and patient. Get ready for Me to reverse his wrongdoings and expose his scheme. You do not have to listen to the father of lies
or allow feelings of shame and guilt to lure you into darkness. I
created you to live and reflect My marvelous light. How I love to
shine through you like a prism, illuminating the beauty of your
soul and magnifying your dreams.

Scriptures
John 5:3; Psalm 18:2; Romans 8:31-39;
Isaiah 43; 1 John 4:4, 15:19

Breakthrough Prayer

Let Your face shine on me. Give me the stamina to push personal barriers out of my life. Your Word decrees, without a doubt, that I am more than an overcomer in You. In Jesus' name. Amen.

BREAKING CURSES AND RELEASING BLESSINGS
Day 82

I decree and declare that the blessing of Abraham is upon me, my family, church, ministry, business, marriage, relationships, and city in Jesus' name.

I destroy and break spirit of envy, jealousy, and anger working against my personal transformation, breakthrough, and revival.

I decree and declare that I arise and declare boldly that this is the year of the Lord.

I destroy and break all demonic monitoring of my life and declare that it be destroyed now in Jesus' name.

I decree and declare that I have been permitted by the Lord to bind and loose what Heaven has already bound and loosed.

I destroy and break every spiritual curse that has been sent seven times against me, and I reverse them and speak sevenfold blessings over those word curses sent.

I decree and declare I am a world changer and glory carrier for the King of kings.

Day 83

Psalm 29:11

*The Lord gives his people strength. The
Lord blesses them with peace.*

God Extends Peace to the Weak

Dream with Me. I know how long it will take to achieve what
is planned for your life. It may seem like an ambitious plan, but is
there anything too hard for Me? Hit the pause button. I'm bringing your dreams, goals, and destiny into total alignment with
Heaven's strategy. My child, don't allow people to rob you of your
peace. Your peace, joy, and righteous in the Holy Spirit is your
kingdom right. Enjoy each day as if it was your first. I am renewing the days of your youth. When you are broken, I will come like
gorilla glue to mend you back together again.

Rest well in knowing that I am resolving those things you felt
could never be solved. I desire to give you peace in a noisy environment. Today, declare that you will walk through doors of opportunity and fulfill your destiny. You are moving from instability
to stability, from lack to abundance, from confusion to eternal
peace, from defeat to victory. Know that every move boldly in
uncertain times will bring you into divine seasons of stability and
reassurance.

Scriptures
Job 33:14; Luke 8:24, 18:27; Jeremiah 32:17;
Philippians 4:7; Mark 4:39

Breakthrough Prayer

Jesus, You are the Prince of peace. Bring peace and harmony over division and chaos to my mind and heart. Let me carry Your peace everywhere I go. In Your name. Amen.

BREAKING CURSES AND RELEASING BLESSINGS
Day 83

I decree and declare that the peace of God rests upon me at all times.

I destroy and break the spirit of shyness and release the roar of Zion within me.

I decree and declare that I will walk in Holy Spirit boldness, peace, and joy.

I destroy and break self-destruction, self-condemnation, self-pity, and low self-esteem in Jesus' name.

I decree and declare that dreams, visions, and God encounters will be evident frequently in my life.

I destroy and break every illegal soul tie that comes at a vulnerable season.

I decree and declare I have what I decree today and will see it established and manifested tomorrow.

I destroy, break, and cast out all spirits of the cankerworm, caterpillar, palmerworm, and locust that would eat up my harvest of blessings, in Jesus' name (see Joel 2:25).

I decree and declare that there is an invisible line drawn in the spirit that will disallow corruption and destruction in my life to cross over.

Day 84

Psalm 30:2-3

*O Lord my God, I cried to you for help,
and you restored my health. You brought
me up from the grave, O Lord. You kept
me from falling into the pit of death.*

God Restores Your Health

Life's demands and pressures can overload your mind and over-work your soul. My child, I will not saddle you with more than you can bear. Cleanse your mind of toxic thinking and worries that want to riddle your heart with doubt, fear, unbelief, and intimidation. I am the Great Physician, and I will not just give you spiritual medicines for pain management or to cope with the pain for the moment but I am your Healer and Miracle Worker. You shall recover and be stronger today than you have ever been. I am causing you to be "healed conscious," and you will be healed. I know things can be overwhelming and too much to take on at one time.

Take a break in My presence, than regroup, champ, to finish what you started. I am bringing balance. You will not stumble into a black hole and fail to complete your mission. Hold on to Me and see victory. My child, remember this is a battle not a skirmish. You are more than a conqueror. You were not created to sit on the sidelines or surrender to defeat. Contend for your passion for Me, health, marriage, and restoration of relationships. Now, take the battlefield knowing that you wage war for peace and righteousness through Christ Jesus!

Scriptures

1 Corinthians 10:13; Jeremiah 30:17;
2 Timothy 1:7; Deuteronomy 28:7; Romans 12:21

Breakthrough Prayer

Jesus, thank You that I don't have to walk in the spirit of fear but faith in You. Strengthen me so that I can walk confidently in the assignment You have given me without taking on unnecessary burdens or unrealistic expectations. Help me to release the pain of the past while providing me with a clear vision and hope for the future. In Jesus' name. Amen.

BREAKING CURSES AND RELEASING BLESSINGS
Day 84

I decree and declare that I am healthy, wealthy in spirit, and strong in my faith.

I destroy and break every viral bacteria, disease, sickness, and illness that comes to plague my body.

I decree and declare that the blood of the Lamb cover and protect my body, mind, and spirit.

I destroy and bind any airborne disease and curse that will try to attach itself to my immune system, in Jesus' name.

I decree and declare that I have the supernatural healing power of the Holy Spirit to bring healing and recovery to those in need.

I destroy and break every disease or sickness that will try to break down my immune system, in Jesus' name,

I decree and declare that this body is the temple of the Holy Spirit and no sickness will come by my dwelling.

Day 85

Psalm 4:8

In peace I will lie down and sleep, for you alone, O Lord, will keep me safe.

God Provides You Rest

Fear not, My royal one. For as you slumbered peacefully through the night, I kept watch over you like a lion guards his pride and territory. I am your Defense, protecting you day and night. My child, know this day that I have cut a pathway in the forest to lead you back to Me if you ever lose your way. Nothing and no one are ever lost or hidden from Me. Just like Joseph went from a pit to the palace, know that I am turning things around for you, too.

Often life's darkest moments offer the greatest opportunities to for your light to brightly shine. Turn yesterday worries into opportunities today for you to believe in Me. Hand over your cares and permit Me to tear down the strongholds holding you back from an abundant life. Don't worry or fret. I have everything under control. Stand back and be amazed. Watch what happens when you obey and I become the Master and Lord of your life.

Scriptures
PSALM 121:5-8, 91:4; PHILIPPIANS 4:6-7; MATTHEW 6:34

Breakthrough Prayer

Drive out the spirit of condemnation, and replace it with healing and wholeness. Show me how to rest in Your presence and glory. When I am weary, make me lie down in green pastures and restore me—my body, mind, and spirit. In Jesus' name, amen.

BREAKING CURSES AND RELEASING BLESSINGS
Day 85

I decree and declare that I shall rest in the presence of God when times are hard for me.

I destroy and break restlessness and sleeplessness in Jesus' name.

I decree and declare that I shall get the rest needed to function properly in my calling.

I destroy and break bad sleeping patterns that cause me to stay awake when I am supposed to be asleep.

I decree and declare that I have a peace of mind and break every pressure that does not belong to me.

I destroy and break every distraction and enemy of my rest in Jesus' name.

I decree and declare that I believe the prophets of God and I will prosper and be successful (see 2 Chron. 20:20).

I destroy and break disorder and confusion within my home, life, church, family, and city.

I decree and declare I will prosper and have peace through the prophets and prophetic ministry (see Ezra 6:14).

I destroy and break every work of satan that is assigned against my life and comes to cause disruption to my destiny, in Jesus' name.

Day 86

Psalm 30:11-12

You have turned my mourning into joyful dancing. You have taken away my clothes of mourning and clothed me with joy, that I might sing praises to you and not be silent. O Lord my God, I will give you thanks forever!

God Rejoices and Dances over You

Recharge yourself this morning with verses that renew your mind and affirm your identity and authority in Jesus. Think on this: What you behold, you become. Challenge yourself to reach new heights personally and professionally. I have wired you with ability and agility to maintain a balanced life. Things do not just happen to us. Change your thoughts and focus all your energy on what I have destined you to do. Disappointments are bound to happen. Just because things did not happen according to your plan doesn't mean they will never happen.

Great minds think alike. Stay connected to great strategists, decision-makers, and planet shakers who will support you in your spiritual and professional development. Godly wisdom leaves a mark on your life that cannot be erased. I declare a break for you, My child, and decree that it is time for a turnaround! I desire to turn your sadness to joy and your frown to a crown worthy of the King of kings. My child, I desire to exchange your cloak of shame for a garment of praise and days of rebellion for righteous living. Do not allow your voice to be drowned out by the nonstop noise of this world. Speak up and make a difference. Let you voice be heard on earth as it is in Heaven.

Scriptures
1 Peter 1:13; Philippians 4:8; Colossians 3:2; Hebrews 3:11; Isaiah 61:3; Acts 18:9; Psalm 83:1

Breakthrough Prayer

Sharpen me like an arrow in Your quiver. Bring together people who will celebrate my growth and accomplishments. Strategically place those who will spur me on to destiny. I want to be active, not passive, so break lethargy off my life and replace it with the spirit of endurance. In Jesus' name, amen.

BREAKING CURSES AND RELEASING BLESSINGS
Day 86

I decree and declare that my praise will release the divine breakthrough that I need.

I destroy and break every work of evil that is sent to discourage me.

I decree and declare that the Lion of the Tribe of Judah will roar out of Zion on my behalf against my enemies.

I destroy and break the powers of the demonic lion packs that come to gang up on me in the spirit.

I decree and declare that I have an arsenal of angelic help that is sent from Heaven to war on my behalf.

I destroy and break the fear of death in Jesus' name.

I decree and declare that I am in right standing with God and have favor with man.

I destroy and break every fetter, chain, or rope that keeps me from receiving my total freedom and breakthrough.

I decree and declare that my dance will bring healing, breakthrough, and sudden joy in my life.

I destroy and break cycles of pain, resentment, and hurt that come when I am lonely, in Jesus' name.

Day 87

Psalm 31:7-8

*I will be glad and rejoice in your unfailing love,
for you have seen my troubles, and you care about
the anguish of my soul. You have not handed me
over to my enemies but have set me in a safe place.*

God Sees Your Troubles

My child, don't let your heart be troubled or anxious about things beyond your control. Remain steadfast and unmovable as you walk with Me. You have a goal to reach and a world to turn. Leave the past behind and chart a new course. Today, declare every sunrise is a sign that today will be brighter and tomorrow's promises await you. Today, declare that past failures, setbacks, and struggles don't define you. God does, and His promises concerning me will surely come to pass. I declare over you, My child, no more delays, setbacks, detours, and hindrances. I am moving you forward into My promised land. You are crossing over to the other side that is flowing with opportunities and no more opposition.

Be that sounding board or stepping stone that propels others into success. I blessed Abraham so that he could turn around and bless others. Open your hands and watch Me pour out blessing after blessing for My name's sake. Align yourself to My kingdom purposes. I will move Heaven and earth to host your dreams. I am your dream catcher as you pitch your ideas, dreams, and desires to Me. Together we will hit a home run of dream fulfillment that will position you to win every time.

Scriptures

PHILIPPIANS 3:14; 2 PETER 1:10; 2 CORINTHIANS 9:8;
PROVERBS 10:22; DEUTERONOMY 28:8

Breakthrough Prayer

Father, how grateful I am that You hold my destiny in Your hands. I confess my sin—wrongdoings, shortcomings, rebellion, missteps, and unforgiveness—and You submerge them in the sea of forgetfulness. You forgive me and erase the sin away. I choose to walk in righteousness and believe what You say about me. Keep me from listening to the enemy's accusations and people's opinions of me. In Jesus' name. Amen.

BREAKING CURSES AND RELEASING BLESSINGS
Day 87

I decree and declare that trouble and violence will be far from me.

I destroy and break every spirit that starts trouble in my sphere of work, activity, or influence.

I decree and declare that I have the anointing to turn a negative environment into a positive one by Word of the Lord.

I destroy and break systems of depression, oppression, and stress that's caused by hardship or hard labor.

I decree and declare that guardian angels are sent to marshal and protect my life, property, and territory.

I destroy and break the spirit of craftiness and cunningness from those I may relate with.

I decree and declare I am complete in Christ and my life is hid with Him in God (see Col. 2:10; 3:3).

I destroy and break the cycle of breakdown, nervous breakdowns, and the spirit of destruction in Jesus' name.

I decree and declare that I live in a realm of peace, joy, love, and happiness (blessings) in Christ.

I destroy and break every ungodly taste, appetite, hunger, and thirst in Jesus' name.

Day 88

Psalm 31:23

*Love the Lord, all you godly ones! For the
Lord protects those who are loyal to him,
but he harshly punishes the arrogant.*

God Loves Your Loyalty

Lighten up today, My child. Do not allow the rollercoaster of
life to turn you inside out. Like a rollercoaster, life has its share of
ups and downs along with dizzying dips and unexpected twists
and hairpin turns. You never ride alone. Today, declare: I will experience God's power in turbulent times. I am courageous in adversity, victorious in battle, and obedient to godly counsel. My
mind is in perfect peace, for the Lord God is on my side.

Staring at a mountain of problems will not make them move.
Talking about your mountain will only magnify the problem. You
have to *speak to* the mountain if you want to see things change.
Words carry great power and potential to change your life. It only
takes a mustard seed of faith to move mountains. Instead of letting
circumstances and situations control you, take control of them.

Scriptures
Psalm 135:14; Jeremiah 1:8, 3:13-14, 39:18;
Matthew 17:20; Luke 17:6; Proverbs 18:21

Breakthrough Prayer

You protect those who are loyal to You and in a covenant relationship with You. Forgive me, Father, for continuing to stare at my circumstances instead of fixing my gaze on You and standing on Your promises. In You, Jesus, I have abundant and fruitful life. In Jesus' name. Amen.

BREAKING CURSES AND RELEASING BLESSINGS
Day 88

I decree and declare that my relationship and loyalty unto the Lord will never be questioned and challenged.

I destroy and disallow any disloyal and uncommitted relationships in my life in Jesus' name.

I decree and declare that I will cross paths with dream chasers, dream catchers, and dream fulfillers.

I destroy and break every pattern of distrust that came as a result of continual letdowns and breaches from others I looked to for help, in Jesus' name.

I decree and declare that I will be a person of my word and will keep my end of the bargain.

I destroy and cut the band of restrainers and command the world's financial system to give up, cough up, lend up, release its wealth and resources that rightfully belong to me and my family, in Jesus' name.

I decree and declare that angels have gone before me to gather up my wealth and resources that are released.

I destroy and break every line of communication from those I have disconnected from who are trying to resurface back in my life.

Day 89

Psalm 31:24

*So be strong and courageous, all you
who put your hope in the Lord!*

God Is Your Great Encourager

Awake, awake My warrior! Despite feeling at times fatigued, I will allow you to weather the storms and conditions of life. Run your race with endurance. Like a long-distance runner, set your gaze at the finish line. Together we are in it to win it. Know that I am your rear guard; encouraging you and propelling you with a final push you needed to break away from the winds of resistance that try to hold you back. Today, declare that you will not lose sight of My promise. Purpose with every step today you will move forward with joy and determination. Fight the good fight. Finish the race. Keep the faith and keep believing.

Your hope rests in knowing that all is well and you are not alone. Just believe. Run your race confident that Jesus will be with you at every turn. Have faith that I will provide supernatural provision, speed, and protection to finish what you started. I come to encourage when you are discouraged. I will become the finishing line to your dream, and you chase Me down to help you fulfill it. You will break every personal record. I will honor you with more favor and glory. You will not be disqualified. I will mantle you with a coat of many colors like Joseph and your dream will carry not only you but leave a mark in the earth.

Scriptures

Isaiah 26:3, 52:12, 58:8; James 4:7;
Ephesians 5:16; Mark 5:36

Breakthrough Prayer

I want my thoughts to glorify You and only You. Renew my mind and sanctify my imagination. When I feel down and out, You encourage my soul. Jesus, You are my hope, joy, and peace. I know that change is coming, but You will help comfort me through it all. Thank You for teaching principles from the Word and showing me how to apply them to live a victorious life.

BREAKING CURSES AND RELEASING BLESSINGS
Day 89

I decree and declare that I shall encourage myself like King David in the Lord.

I destroy and disallow any words of negativity, slander, and gossip in my life, family, church, leadership, ministry, business, and divine relationships.

I decree and declare that I have the faith required to remove every mountain in my life and rebuke every storm as well.

I destroy and break every spirit of agony, distress, hurt, pain, regret, and bitterness in Jesus' name.

I decree and declare that I have the courage and faith to climb mountains and take faith risks.

I destroy and break every power of guilt that comes back from the past in Jesus' name.

I decree and declare that the prophetic calling and work is stirring up on the inside of me to bring change to my generation.

I destroy and break any spirit of the traitor that would attempt to connect with me or those with whom I relate.

I decree and declare that everything that God has entrusted me with will have longevity.

I destroy and break every demonic spirit of hate, malice, and criticism that comes in my life, in Jesus' name.

Day 90

Psalm 32:7-8

For you are my hiding place; you protect me from trouble. You surround me with songs of victory. The Lord says, "I will guide you along the best pathway for your life. I will advise you and watch over you."

God Shows You His Way

Awake, child of Mine. I have your best interests in mind and know the direction you should take today. Allow Me to be your roadmap, pinpointing places of promise and setting your priorities. Eventually, you reach a crossroad. Time to make a choice—stay the course or venture into something new. Today, declare that you will respond in faith and follow where the Holy Spirit leads. "I am always in the right place at the right time because God orders my steps. My purpose here is priceless—turning people's hearts to God and not storing up things that can be stolen, lose value, or destroyed."

My child, I've heard your prayers and will release healing of deep hurts and recovery from great loss. The unjust will have their day in My courts, while the just will walk in undeniable favor, grace, and peace. I am piecing back together your shattered dreams. Through this hardship, you learned patience, perseverance, and endurance. You will encounter persecution for My name's sake. I am strengthening you from the inside out. I will give you the courage and boldness of a lion.

Scriptures

2 Peter 1:21, 3:16; Jeremiah 29:11, 30:17;
Proverbs 4:23, 28:1; Psalm 32:1, 71:20; 2 Timothy 2:3-5;
1 Samuel 17:20, 37; Isaiah 54:1-3

Breakthrough Prayer

Father, I totally surrender my will to Yours. I turn my life decisions over to You. My eyes have not seen, my ears have not heard all that You have planned for me. You have marked out my spiritual journey—and desire for me to finish strong.

BREAKING CURSES AND RELEASING BLESSINGS
Day 90

I decree and declare that I will find and discover my own original purpose in Christ for my generation.

I destroy and break demonic traffic and roadblocks that are set up by the enemy to cause frustration to my destination.

I decree and declare that I have the compass of the Holy Spirit and I have clear direction to where I am supposed to be in Jesus' name.

I destroy, break, and disallow anything that would suddenly bring accident, tragedy, collisions, and damage to the work that God has given to my charge, in Jesus' name.

I decree and declare that I am insured and covered by the angels of the Lord.

I destroy, break, and remove every blockage to my vision and every cracked or shattered windshield to my purpose, in Jesus' name.

I decree and declare that Jesus is the vehicle driver of my destiny and we together are excelling to our destination.

I destroy and cancel premature death and injuries caused by demonic attacks.

I decree and declare that my life is guarded by the hosts of angels summoned at Jesus' command.

I destroy and break every evildoer who is sent against my season of transition and declare that I am in my due season in Jesus' name.

ABOUT DR. HAKEEM COLLINS

Dr. Hakeem Collins is a new prophetic voice and governmental minister with a unique anointing in the prophetic, healings, and the supernatural. He is a sought-after conference speaker, produces a weekly radio program called "The VOICE," and author of *Born to Prophesy* and *Heaven Declares*. He is CEO of Champions International based in Wilmington, Delaware, where he resides. To learn more about his ministry, please visit www.hakeemcollinsministries.com.

FREE E-BOOKS?
YES, PLEASE!

Get **FREE** and deeply discounted **Christian books** for your **e-reader** delivered to your inbox **every week!**

IT'S SIMPLE!

VISIT lovetoreadclub.com

SUBSCRIBE by entering your email address

RECEIVE free and discounted e-book offers and inspiring articles delivered to your inbox every week!

Unsubscribe at any time.

SUBSCRIBE NOW!

LOVE TO READ CLUB

visit **LOVETOREADCLUB.COM** ▶